FISHING THE
FOUR SEASONS

FISHING THE
FOUR SEASONS

DAVE HUGHES

THE LYONS PRESS

Guilford, Connecticut
An imprint of The Globe Pequot Press

The Lyons Press is an imprint of The Globe Pequot Press.

Cover photograph by Tim Irwin.
Other photography by Tom Montgomery (pages 8, 32, 76, 116), Scott Ripley (page 2), Jim Schollmeyer (pages 52/53, 126/127).

Illustrations by Rod Walinchus.
FRONTISPIECE: *Rainbow trout taken on a dry fly.*

Printed in the United States of America

10 9 8 7 6 5 4 3 2 1

The Library of Congress Cataloging-in-Publication Data is available on file.

CONTENTS

LEFTY'S PREFACE

Many fly fishermen would love to live the life of Dave Hughes. I asked him how often he goes fishing. "Oh, not often enough," he said. "I guess maybe a hundred days a year." Think about that! More than one day out of four, Dave is on the water, almost always fishing for trout. A lot of people I know would enjoy even half that much time on the stream.

Dave has been an active outdoor writer for 17 years. Many of today's outdoor writers have gone to school and learned to write, then spent some time on the stream, then started writing about fly fishing. The lack of real on-the-water time shows in their writing. But this is not true of Dave, who is a superb writer. He won the Pete Hidy Memorial Award for Literary Achievement, which is given none too freely by the Fly Fishers Club of Oregon.

He is on the staff of *Fly Rod and Reel* magazine as their "Fly Fishing Success" columnist — which means he is writing about technique, something he knows a great deal about. Dave has mostly concentrated on experiencing and writing on trout fishing. Few anglers come close to what he's accomplished.

He is the author of 16 books and there are more coming. Here are just a few of his published titles: *American Fly Tying Manual; Western Streamside Guide; Deschutes; Yellowstone River and its Angling;* plus the four-book *Strategies for Streams* series. These books have improved the fishing of thousands of fly rodders.

Dave is a rather quiet and unassuming guy. It takes a little time to discover his great sense of humor. But he's a man well worth knowing. He is committed to the conservation of our resources and, in fact, was founding president of the conservation organization Oregon Trout. And he was awarded the Lew Jewett Memorial Life Membership in the Federation of Fly Fishers.

Read and study this book, and you will know how to fish trout throughout the year.

Bernard "Lefty" Kreh
Hunt Valley, Maryland

OVERLEAF: *Icy angling on the upper Snake River, Wyoming.*

CHAPTER ONE

WINTER

Winter is the dead end of the fishing year, right? It's a time for fiddling with tackle, repairing it from the last season and preparing it for the next.

Most folks look at winter in that same timeworn way. It's not necessarily wrong. Any time is a good time to keep your gear operational so you can grab it and go fishing. Winter days are short; you're smart to use a few of those long, dark hours to make what repairs you must. But you're also smart to disregard the old cliché that declares winter fit only for tinkering with tackle. Instead, take advantage of the many opportunities winter offers to get out on the water and put that tackle into play against trout.

If you look at winter correctly, it's not the dead end of the last season, but the birth of the next.

OPPORTUNITIES WHEN THE WEATHER IS WINTRY

Rick Hafele called last January. "I'm restless," he said. "Let's go fish the Deschutes."

I looked out my window and watched the weather snort. A storm had played around Portland for a couple of days. "Right," I said.

"I'm serious," he insisted. "The weather will be better over the mountains. Fishing will be great."

The Deschutes River is across the Cascade Range from Portland. Storms drop most of their moisture and exhaust their energy climbing the steep west slopes of the mountains. Things can be more peaceful in winter on the river side of the range. They can also be far colder.

"You think it'll be warm enough to fish over there?" I asked.

"I think so," Rick said. "And if it isn't, we'll have a trip, anyway." That's often enough reason to go fishing in winter, so we went.

Rick was right about the fishing, which is not unusual. He has a master's degree in the study of trout-stream insects. He's written a couple of books about trout fishing. He's also the talent in the video, *Anatomy of a Trout Stream*. But Rick was wrong about the weather. It was windy and bitter on *both* sides of the mountains.

The Deschutes is a big, brawling river, tumbled with lava and rocks and rapids. It doesn't have many meanders, and it never pauses to rest in pools. It can seem a formidable river until you realize you can nibble at its edges and catch trout. That's especially true in winter, and on any river, not just the Deschutes.

Think about any stream you might want to fish in winter. Envision its flows, and think about what I'll call its *soft spots*, where the water remains relatively deep but the current is gentle. On the Deschutes, this happens only in eddies and at the edges. On your home stream, it might happen more often in pools or in deep runs. Wherever it happens, and trout aren't forced to fight constant current, that's where you'll find fish in winter.

When we reached the river, Rick Hafele opened his nymph box, revealing row after row of flies that averaged #14 and #16. It reminded me of the most common mistake made in winter fishing, one I used to make myself. I assumed trout would be unlikely to move for something tiny, even if they

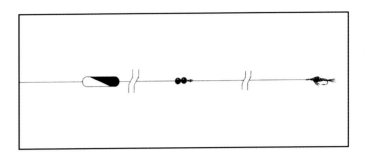

Rigging for Winter Nymphing — Split-Shot and Indicator

happened to see it, which didn't seem likely. Rick scolded me out of that notion in a streamside lecture long ago.

"Most aquatic insect nymphs and larvae are in their earliest instars all through winter," he told me. "Trout are used to seeing and eating tiny bites. Show them a large nymph, and it's something they haven't had a chance at since last summer. They don't take it."

Rick was right about that, too. By switching from nymphs that averaged #10 and #12 to nymphs in sizes #14 and #16, I began showing trout what they eat all the time, especially in winter. I suddenly started catching many more fish, and not just at that time of year. Reduce the size nymphs you fish all year long, and you're likely to catch more fish and larger ones, not fewer and smaller.

The next step for rigging in winter, after selecting a small nymph, is to select equipment that allows you to fish deep and slow, not high and fast. That usually means *split-shot and indicator nymphing.* Stout tackle — 9 to 9 1/2-foot rods balanced to cast 6 and 7-weight lines — will do the job fine. That's what most people use in winter, but in truth, such heavy tackle is not necessary.

Rick Hafele's primary nymphing rod, winter and summer, is an 8-foot graphite for a double-taper floating 4-weight line.

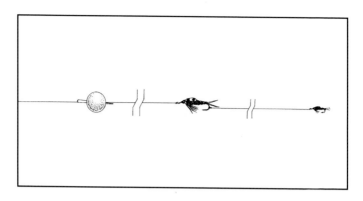

Rigging for Winter Nymphing — Two Nymphs and Indicator

And he's the best all-around nymph fisherman I know. My own favorite outfit is an 8 1/2-foot graphite rod for a double-taper floating 5-weight line. That's closer to fine than it is to heavy. But it propels split-shot, indicators, and weighted nymphs as far as I need to toss them in winter — 20 to 40 feet. It also allows a quick switch to tiny dry flies if the opportunity to fish a winter hatch arises.

I watched while Rick knotted a standard nymphing leader, tapered and 10 feet long, to his floating line. In place of split-shot, he tied a heavily weighted #8 generic salmon-fly nymph to the end of his tippet and tied a #16 nymph on an 18-inch dropper from the hook bend. He slid a buoyant and bright strike indicator two feet from his line tip.

This rig prepared Rick to fish deep and slow, which is critical to winter nymphing. It also allowed him to offer the trout a choice between the large fly and the small one, a step he took only because the Deschutes is home to lots of giant salmon-fly nymphs. But Rick knew that even if the trout had no particular interest in such a large nymph, the fly was providing enough weight to get his other, smaller fly to the bottom of the river where trout could find it.

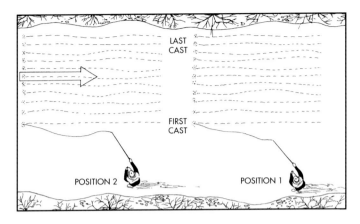

Covering Water When Nymphing

Rick began probing a slow run alongside the main current. His first cast was nearly straight upstream. His nymphs plummeted to the bottom. He tended the drift with mends and rolls to allow his indicator to float freely downstream, just as a dry fly might. Then he could be sure that the nymphs were being dangled just as naturally along the bottom. They ticked rocks now and then, or Rick would have added a shot or two.

Rick's second and subsequent casts were a foot or two out into the current from the previous line of drift. On each cast, his nymphs painted a brushstroke along a parallel bit of bottom. In this way, he showed his flies to any fish that were holding in the water he was able to reach in short casts from his first casting position. Then Rick waded upstream to a second casting position to cover another section of the streambed with another sequence of parallel drifts.

I stood on shore and watched Rick fish, chatting all the while. It's a great way to absorb all you can from somebody who is an expert at a certain kind of fishing. Watch him rig, then distract him with drivel while he fishes that rig. If he has some success, note precisely what he did to make it happen.

It's an excellent way to learn, and the more you learn the more trout you'll catch at any time of year.

I watched while Rick moved up to explore a slow run that was about four feet deep. He adjusted his indicator up the leader a foot before he began setting his hook against slight hesitations in the drift of his indicator. Most of the time those hesitations were the bottom. A few times they were not. He prodded half a dozen redside rainbows into the air and led them to his hand before he finished that run, hooking them all on his #16 fly. Two of them were 18 inches long and close to three pounds.

Rick moved a few hundred feet upstream to fish the soft edge of another run, making a few adjustments in his rigging before things became right. Then even I, from my distant conversational position on the bank, saw his indicator dart down and dash upstream.

Rick raised his rod to set the hook and was tight to a steelhead. I'd like to report that the fight was astonishing. But the fish was small, just six pounds, and a little lethargic. Rick led it to his hand a while later, pried the #8 nymph from its jaw, and admired the fish before releasing it. That's when I realized why he'd used that large fly rather than split-shot to get his smaller fly to the bottom where it would tempt trout.

He'd been hoping for a steelhead from the moment we'd left Portland.

Streamers, not nymphs, have historically been the fly of choice for fishing in winter, on the assumption that trout will chase something only if it's big. Actually, trout are not anxious to chase anything in the cold water of winter, but a streamer fished right can fool trout in certain types of water.

The best water for streamers in winter is deep and pooled to near stillness. Trout gather down in the darkness. You can retrieve a streamer through them, but it's tough to fish a nymph where there is little current to escort it along.

Never force winter trout to pursue any fly down to its death. Your goal should be to deliver a streamer slowly and as close to the trout's lie as you can get it. With that goal in mind, you'll have no trouble figuring out how to rig for streamer fishing and how to present your flies to pooled winter fish.

Winter pools are the place for medium gear; stout won't hurt. I use an 8 1/2-foot rod loaded with a weight-forward 6-weight sinking-tip line if the stream is small and its pools are less than six feet deep. If the pools are deeper, I go to a wet-belly or full 30-foot ultra-fast-sinking line. A 7 or 8-weight outfit would work better for large pools, but I stick with the 6-weight because I don't want to trot back to my pickup for a different rod every time I encounter a larger or smaller pool.

Because I use relatively light gear, I cast small streamers — #8 and #10. Trout seem pleased enough to accept them. If you catch me bundled up and launching long casts over deep pools in winter, you'll catch me with a #8 or #10 olive or black Woolly Bugger tied to my tippet. It will be weighted with 15 to 20 turns of lead wire the diameter of the hook shank.

The most effective winter streamer retrieve is best illustrated by a trip I took with Rick Hafele and Scott Richmond to an Oregon tailwater, the Malheur River. This river is small. Its pools are an easy cast across, six to eight feet deep. It holds scattered populations of browns that are large enough to make winter fishing worthwhile.

We went there in December. The sun was bright but weakly warm during the short days. At night the air was so cold it snapped. Rim ice formed half an inch thick and several feet out from the edges of the pools by morning. The sun failed to melt much of it by mid-afternoon, which was when we dared tiptoe out and enter the water.

I recall one pool in particular. Rick fished where the slight current entered the head of the pool. There was enough flow to keep the water from freezing, so he did not have to break

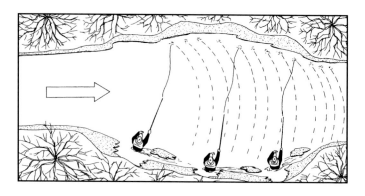

Covering the Water of a Pool in Winter with a Fanned Series of Casts from an Icy Shore

ice to get to his fishing. Scott, also an author of a couple of fishing books and an expert in his own right, fished the center of the pool where the current slowed and a few feet of quarter-inch ice had developed around the edges. I fished the foot of the pool, where the water slowed and slid between shelves of half-inch ice. Unfortunately for me, the open water was 15 feet of ice from shore. I had to break a lead to get there.

When I got to where I could reach the open water, I was waist deep and still iced in. I'd make a cast, then break off a plate of ice and shove it out of the way so I could move down the pool a couple of feet while the wet-tip line tugged the Woolly Bugger to the bottom. Then I'd set my feet and inch the fly along the bottom with the slowest hand-twist retrieve I could manage.

I cracked ice and gradually worked my way down the edge of the pool. The lead of open water narrowed to 30 feet. On half the retrieves, weeds plucked at the fly and I had to clean it off before casting again, which didn't do anything to warm my numb fingers. On one cast I felt weeds tug, tried to lift the fly, and felt it tug sullenly back.

I brought the fish in as swiftly as I could, which was not swiftly at all because it was a brown of about four pounds. Rick and Scott gathered to watch me remove the #10 olive Woolly Bugger from the trout's lip. I slid the fish into the water, slipped my wet hands deep into the warmth of my waders, backed out of the icy water, and became a spectator, while Rick and Scott returned to their own parts of the frigid pool and used the same creeping streamer retrieve to work more magic on trout of similar size.

WINTER HATCHES WHEN THE WEATHER IS WARM

I have an early February note in my logs from last year for the Crooked River in central Oregon. It says the water was clear and cold, 38 degrees F. It also says the air warmed in the afternoon to 45 degrees. There were ice layers four inches thick in the backwaters but no ice in the riffles and runs entering the pools that held the many trout for which the Crooked is so well known.

This note claims a 50-fish day, which I'm forced to believe because I was there when I caught them. How did that happen in the deep freeze of winter? It's easy to explain: The sun warmed the water in late afternoon, a midge hatch came off, trout rose to feed on the midges, and I found the right fly to match them and fool the fish.

These kinds of days happen so often in winter that I've learned to anticipate them. It takes no more than a quick scan of weather reports for predictions of 45-degree highs. Fishing will be good if the weather is reasonable, so long as afternoon temperatures creep up near that magic number. Fishing will be even better if you get that relative warmth along with a cloud cover and a soft rain. Then the hatches can start in early afternoon and go on for hours.

On warm winter days, when you anticipate a hatch, you read the water by watching for rises. But don't waste time looking for them in rough riffles and runs. Look on the surface of those same soft spots where you found fish on cold winter days: where the current slows, or even eddies back on itself, right along the edges of the stream.

Insects that emerge in cold weather are almost always small. Trout rise to take them very quietly, showing with the tiniest of dimples. You must watch the water carefully to spot them. Be patient. Be watchful. Get as close to the water as you can. I always carry miniature binoculars when I'm fishing and sometimes use them to scan water a scant 15 to 20 feet away.

With binoculars, if you follow a drifting midge or mayfly dun on its chilly winter cruise, you might notice that it has suddenly, unaccountably disappeared. That's how subtly trout can rise in winter. You must be watchful for the insects in the first place and for their uneventful exit in the second.

Winter hatches are pretty much the same all across the continent — East, West, and everywhere in between. You'll always see a few little brown stones and tiny winter black stones, in #14 and #16. These look like pepper sprinkled onto streamside snowbanks. They often lose their grip on the snow and tumble over the edge. Sometimes — watch carefully! — you'll see trout sipping at the interface of water and snow-covered banks. These fish are usually feeding on winter stonefly hatches.

The best flies to match them are downwing dries such as Polly Rosborough's Little Brown Stone and Jim Schollmeyer's Deer-Hair Caddis. Use them in #14 and #16. The nymphs of these insects are also busy in winter, near the edges because that's where they crawl out to emerge. If dry flies fail you, which will not happen often if the fish are rising visibly, you can usually catch a few fish on Sylvester Nemes' Partridge & Orange soft-hackle in #12 or #14.

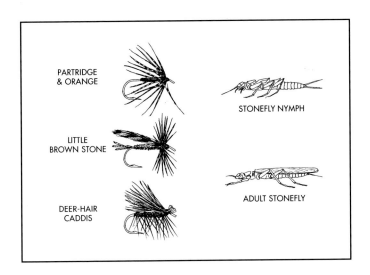

PARTRIDGE & ORANGE

STONEFLY NYMPH

LITTLE BROWN STONE

ADULT STONEFLY

DEER-HAIR CADDIS

Fly Patterns for Early Stonefly Hatches

Fish the dries on 6X-tippets. Place short, delicate casts to the gentle rises and you'll trick your fish nearly every time. If you switch to the soft-hackled wet, make cross-stream casts that coax it through the rises on a slow swing. When you feel a take, keep yourself from jerking; let the trout set the hook itself. Rear back against the fine tippet and you'll merely break off, unless the trout is too small to be worth catching.

Midges are the most common fare on warmish winter days. They can be as large as #14 or #16; more often they're #18 or #20. You'd think trout would not get enough nutrition out of these insects to make them worth the energy expended. But this isn't true. Trout take up stations in gentle water, then tip up and down, inhaling midges while wasting little effort.

A hatch of black midges fueled my 50-fish day in February on the Crooked River. They hatched on a tailout and were delivered down a short and gentle riffle into the pool below. Trout from the entire length of the pool gathered to greet them.

The rise rings of their takes were so soft I nearly waded right past them, but a projecting snout caught my eye. I watched a while and finally realized I was seeing a school of fish feeding on a fleet of stranded midges.

This was such exciting news that I began fishing with what I'd been using, a #16 Adams Parachute tied to a 5X-tippet. That's a fine combination to explore for fish with but it was far too large to impress those midging trout.

After flailing awhile with the parachute, I took time to capture a midge in the aquarium net I always carry for just such moments. The midge was black, #20. I added three feet of 6X-tippet and then tied on a #20 Sangre de Cristo Midge, an emerger pattern that has a black dubbed body, split white Micro-Fibette tails, and a few turns of grizzly hackle wrapped around a white foam wing post that is clipped short.

I cast this fly 20 feet to the nearest rises. I could not see it on the water but did see a slight circle form where I suspected it might be. I raised the rod and brought up the first rainbow of that winter season. It wasn't any giant. But a trout willing to sip my dry fly doesn't have to be big to loom large in my eyes when four inches of ice are in the backwaters.

I use just a few flies to take trout during winter midge hatches. The most important, to me, is that Sangre de Cristo parachute emerger in #16 to #22. It takes fish sipping in the film. I also use a palmered Adams Midge, in #16 to #20, to imitate single or clustered midges tangled and afloat on the surface. The Griffith's Gnat, in #16 to #22, imitates either an adult or an emerger, and I'd never be without a few of them.

The midge pupa itself has often been overlooked, but not by Sylvester Nemes. His Syl's Midge soft-hackle in #16 and #18 matches it. It has a peacock herl body and a turn of gray partridge hackle. That's it. Fish the pattern on a gentle swing inches deep to trout rising to midges, and you'll be surprised how often trout accept it after refusing dries.

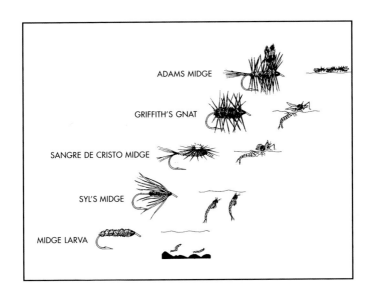

ADAMS MIDGE

GRIFFITH'S GNAT

SANGRE DE CRISTO MIDGE

SYL'S MIDGE

MIDGE LARVA

Fly Patterns for Midges

The Midge Larva is the final fly on my list of imitations. It is tied in #16 to #20 and has a peacock herl body ribbed with copper wire. I suspect trout take this for a pupa just launching off the bottom rather than for a larva. Fix the fly to a three-foot 6X-tippet, then tie a tiny yarn indicator at the tippet knot. If necessary, a single micro-shot will get the fly down to bottom-feeding fish. In shallow water, I often fish this larval pattern in shallow water to trout that are winking visibly. I cast it upstream and fish it dead-drift, again as if fishing the indicator as a dry fly.

During winter hatches of little olive mayflies, I do the opposite and fish the dry fly as an indicator. It's difficult to tell which stage of the little olive trout prefer, emerger or dun. Some trout take one, some the other. Sometimes two trout will feed side by side on insects in different life-cycle stages, so it's wise to offer both on the same cast.

Little olives, or *Baetis,* begin hatching in January during a mild year and continue clear into December, which is winter again. Their heaviest hatches are in February, March, and April, then in September, October, and November. They're the first major mayfly hatch of the year.

Little olives, like midges, are tiny and difficult to spot, and the rises they prompt are subtle. But trout are eager for them, and you need to be aware of them to be a successful early-season fly fisherman.

It's a mistake to think that little olives come in only one color. The same species will vary from pale green to blackish olive, sometimes on the same stream. A single species can vary from #16 down to #22. And there are a couple dozen species scattered across North America.

I used to believe that one right fly would match a hatch on all waters in all conditions. I now know that the best way to match any hatch anywhere is to carry three or four pattern styles in a narrow range of sizes and colors. This is especially true for the little olives.

When I fish *Baetis* mayfly hatches, I insist on fishing dry flies or emergers awash in the film. I have done well in the past fishing Pheasant Tail Nymphs, in #16 to #20, before and during hatches of little olives. If you want to do that, rig a small indicator and add a micro-shot or two; you'll outfish me. But I prefer to fish the surface with a combination of two flies, one for the dun and one for the emerger.

I use the same #16 to #20 Sangre de Cristo emerger that I described for midges earlier, except in olive instead of black. This is tied to a 20-inch tippet of 6X or 7X, which is clinch-knotted to the bend of the dry fly I'm using to imitate the dun. I've seen times when the dun served only as a marker for constant takes to this emerger.

I've seen other times when trout ignored the emerger and took the dry fly for the dun exclusively. It usually requires

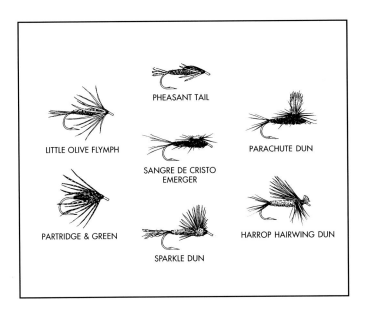

Fly Patterns for Little Olive Hatches

some experimentation to find the right dun pattern. That's why I carry several, each tied in #16 to #22 and in two shades of olive, light and dark.

The first style, and often the best, is the Sparkle Dun, tied with a Z-lon tail to represent the trailing nymphal shuck, a fur body, and flared deer-hair wing. I also use a Parachute Dun, tied with split dun tails, fur body, gray polypro wingpost, and dark dun hackle. The Harrop Hairwing Dun, with split dun tails, olive fur body, dun hackle, and natural deer-hair wing, also takes lots of trout for me during *Baetis* hatches.

When trout refuse all dries and emergers offered during little olive hatches, I try a couple of wets. I reserve the perversity to use wet flies and to tip up my goatish nose at using nymphs during a little olive hatch. I can't explain my own behavior. But I can explain the success of Sylvester Nemes'

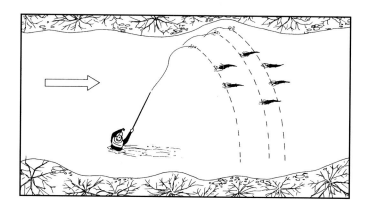

Fishing Wets to Rising Trout

Partridge & Green and Pete Hidy's Little Olive Flymph during hatches of *Baetis* mayflies.

Lots of these little duns get stranded during emergence in cold weather. Trout take them underwater. A soft-hackle imitation should be tied with an olive silk body and two turns of gray partridge hackle. The Flymph is dressed with dun hackle fiber tails, gold tinsel rib, rough olive fur body, and dun hen hackle wound over the front half of the body. Both are tied in #16 to #20.

To fish the wets, just nip off the dry fly and tie on the wet. Fish the fly down and around, on a gentle swing. If trout are rising, swim the wet right through their rise rings. If they're not, prospect wherever the water is marked by current seams, gravel shelves, and boulder lies.

It's no secret that mayflies hatch best on those days with a cloud cover, and a soft rain falling. If the rain turns to snow, so what? The insects don't seem to be bothered unless it's accompanied by a blitz of wind. And everybody knows that trout don't have the sense to come in out of the weather. Why should you, when winter trout rise right through it?

I'd be lying if I told you I spend a lot of time prowling stillwaters in winter. Warm water sinks toward the bottom when temperatures hang around freezing. Trout sink with the slight warmth and become rather dormant in winter. You can catch them if you rig right and are patient enough. But it's not the most fun you'll find throughout the four seasons of the trout fishing year.

You can catch an occasional trout, even have a rare exciting day, on stillwaters that remain free of ice through the winter. Trout will be down near the bottom, but not on it, because organic decay uses up most oxygen on the bottom itself. You must rig to fish the water just *above* the bottom. Trout won't make fast moves. Explore with your fly very slowly.

By now you've figured out the formula for stillwater trout in winter: fish deep and slow. Choose a line that fishes the correct depth in the water you've chosen. I use a shooting-head system: the fast-sinking head for water six to 10 feet deep, extra-fast for depths 10 to 15 feet down, and ultra-fast for water 15 to 25 feet. If trout are below that, they're safe from me. But there's no reason you couldn't fish a lead-core head and drape it down into the abyssal depths if you wanted to. Let me know how you do.

Having chosen a line to get down, you next decide what fly to fish. I offer the trout a choice by rigging a weighted streamer trailed by an unweighted nymph. Since a Woolly Bugger looks like lots of lake food forms, I'll usually use one in black or olive, #6 or #8. The aquatic insects that survive in the greatest abundance on the oxygen-poor bottom are midge larvae, so my choice for a nymph is a midge pattern, the TDC, in #14 or #16.

Keep your leader to the streamer four or five feet long and the dropper to the nymph about 18 inches or so. That will

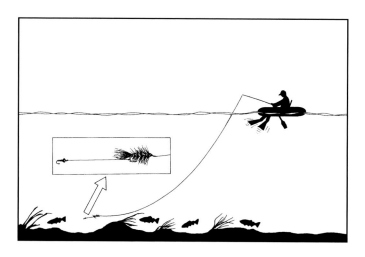

Trolling for Stillwater Trout in Winter with a Two-Nymph Rig

keep both of the flies traveling at the depths reached by your sinking line.

The only problem left is getting the fly combination down to the water just above the bottom. You can cast and count if you'd like. Cast long. Count slowly. Add five seconds to each subsequent cast until you tick weeds or the bottom itself. Shorten the count just a few seconds on the next cast, then prepare for the tedium of casting and retrieving into numbness and beyond.

What I'd rather do is make a single cast out behind my pram (or my float tube, if I can dress warmly enough to stand the water). After giving the line time to coax the flies deep, I row or flipper slowly away.

Trolling has advantages over casting and retrieving in winter. You show your fly to all sorts of areas in the lake. Stillwater trout tend to school up, so towing your enticement around increases the chances you'll run across them. You also keep your hands dry; constant casting and retrieving means wet, cold hands. By trolling, you keep your flies continually patrolling the depths inhabited by trout.

That's all I've got to say about probing the depths of lakes and ponds for trout in winter. If you've got the patience to slug it out with the weather, you'll likely get a chance to slug it out with some trout as well. If that happens, it's likely they'll be large ones.

A few stillwater hatches occur in winter, especially on 45-degree days and warmer in late February and early March. When these hatches take place, trout respond. Obviously, if you notice trout rising, you should fish for them with imitations of what they're eating.

Winter hatches are nearly always midges in stillwaters. I've already given my favorite patterns for them earlier in this chapter and won't repeat them here. Consider, however, that stillwater midges are often larger than their stream cousins and appear in a wider array of colors. For lake fishing, you'll want to carry midge patterns in #12, #14, #16, and #18, in black, tan, green, and red. That will cover almost anything you'll encounter.

To fish winter hatches, get out your fine gear and cast to the rises. It's often difficult to tell whether trout are sipping pupae on the rise, emergers in the film, or adults on top. Therefore, it's a good idea to offer a dry or emerger at the end of three feet of 5X or 6X-tippet, and a pupa pattern that is tied to a two-foot dropper of 6X or 7X. If you begin catching trout on one fly and not the other, nip off the one that's not working; this will reduce tangles.

Trout aren't the only critters that feed on winter midges. Backswimmers, large and predatory insects that hang out in open water, also enjoy nibbling at them. Trout, given a chance, nibble at the backswimmers. If you see winter rises that appear too big and too brutal to bring about the death of a mere midge, assume trout are feeding on backswimmers feeding

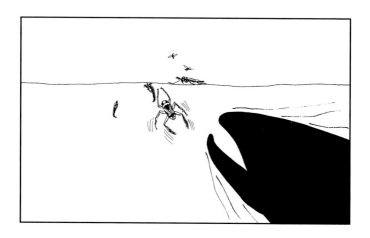

Trout Feeding on Backswimmers Feeding on Midges

on midges. Tie a #10 or #12 Prince Nymph or Coachman wet to a 5X-tippet. Cast it out, give it scant seconds to sink, then retrieve it with fast strips.

Backswimmers dash boldly along on the hunt, traveling just beneath the surface. A nymph or wet fly fished with a rapid retrieve will often get whacked hard. That's why you want a reasonably sturdy tippet when you fish this way on lakes and ponds in the late stages of winter; big trout hitting hard can part fragile tippets in a hurry.

WINTER PREPARATION

I don't have a lot to tell you about dressing for winter fishing that you can't figure out for yourself. Wear lots of clothes and put them on in layers so you can peel them off in the event that you encounter unexpected warmth. That same warmth will prompt the trout to rise; you can expect to be dressed most comfortably when fishing is best.

Make your inner layer of thin polypro and the layers outside that either thick polypro or wool. Avoid cotton clothes in winter, especially beneath waders. Cotton captures moisture. When you take your waders off at the end of the day, if you've been wearing cotton you'll catch a chill and perhaps a cold. Your outer layer should be a coat or jacket that is both windproof and waterproof.

Make your winter waders neoprenes. For winter wading, boot-foot waders are best because they are looser on your feet. If you wear stocking-foot waders with wading brogues over them, be sure the brogues are big enough for two or three pairs of socks without binding. If your normal brogues are even slightly tight, your single purchase to prepare for winter fishing should be an extra set of wading shoes, a size larger than those you normally wear.

A stocking cap is handy to have in the back of your vest or in your boat bag. Tug it over your ears before they begin to get chilled. A wool or polypro muffler wound around your neck can add degrees of warmth that will surprise you if you haven't tried one.

I consider fingerless wool gloves an essential for winter fishing. They leave your fingers free to tie on flies and new tippets while warming the complication of ligaments in the backs of your hands, which is what keeps your fingers nimble. I like a wading jacket with wool or pile-lined pockets I can jam my hands into. It doesn't hurt to have a handwarmer hidden in there, which perhaps might be your wisest second purchase for winter fishing.

No matter what you wear to keep you warm in winter, it won't help at all if you get it wet. Add an extra element of caution in all of your wading. Simply do not take any chances that might result in a dunking. Things are twice, perhaps even three times, as dangerous out there in winter around water. Be cautious. Use a wading staff in fast water. Never get wet.

I carry a waterproof case full of stick matches plus a few fire-starter sticks in my vest in winter. I've not yet really needed them. But I have plunked myself down on a few cottonwood islands around lunchtime and built warming fires. The comfort of the fire is fine, but finer still is the comfort of knowing that if I ever truly needed a fire, those small items and my practice using them would make it possible for me to get one going in an actual emergency.

DISTANT WINTER OPPORTUNITIES

Modern life offers options you should exercise now and then, though they might require a bit more expenditure of that condensation of effort we call money. So if you live in an area that doesn't offer much reward for time spent fishing in winter, then you might be wise to save a little on other expenses and reward yourself with a winter trip to someplace where it's warm.

The prime example of such a place is the San Juan River tailwater down in New Mexico. In winter the weather is not precisely like summer, but it's usually not bad compared to where you were when you took off to go there. Trout in the San Juan can always be coaxed to nymphs fished deep, on the rare days when they're not nipping at midges or *Baetis* mayflies on top.

Many similar spots throughout the South and Southwest provide excellent fishing all winter long. Consider them. They are only a plane ride away.

The Southern Hemisphere is not so near, also not so cheap. When it's winter up here, however, it's guaranteed to be summer down there. I've fished Chile, Argentina, and New Zealand. And I've found that half the fun of fishing those remote lands is doing it in weather a world away from winter.

The other half is the great fishing itself, over trout that are large and often visible.

The final half of the fun you get from fishing the opposite hemisphere is the sure sense of exploration you're going to get in those new geographies and cultures.

That adds up to three halves, which gives you an idea how the fun of those distant adventures gets magnified.

OVERLEAF: *Scott Schnebly and a young client at Warm Springs Creek in central Idaho.*

CHAPTER TWO

SPRING

I fished in northern New Mexico a couple of seasons ago with Craig Martin, author of *Fly Fishing Northern New Mexico* (Sangre de Cristo Fly Fishers, 1991). I'd always wanted to fish the Rio Grande in the canyon west of Taos. But that river was a storm of muddy water.

We drove to a trailhead high in the nearby Rockies, hopped aboard mountain bikes, and flew down a trail still laced dangerously with snowbanks. We arrived shaken but safe alongside a tiny stream that had obviously not been fished by anyone else that year. It was not yet knocked out by snowmelt because not much snow had melted that high in the mountains.

We were able to take quite a few Paiute cutthroat that looked like knife blades of gold when held in the hand. They were not large, but considering the size of the stream they came from, they were not that small either. We returned them.

While Craig and I rested at the car after a hellacious huff up the same trail we'd dashed down earlier, Craig said something that helped me, and I hope will help you, get a fix on spring trout fishing.

"By the time the Rio Grande gets into good shape to fish," he said, "this stream will be unfishable."

"One goes out when the other comes in?" I asked.

"That's half the challenge of fishing in the spring around here. It's as much fun finding a stream that's in shape to fish as it is catching the fish once you've found it." That sums up spring trout fishing. You will invest as much time finding water where conditions for fishing are right as you will fishing once you're where you want to be.

In most of the temperate ranges where trout thrive, spring conditions can be divided into three parts: pre-runoff, spate season, and post-runoff. In any given area, it's likely that different streams will be in pre-runoff, spate, and post-runoff condition at the same time. If you take time to find a stream — or a tailwater, spring creek, or lake — that's fishing the way you want it, you won't need to battle the high and muddy water that is considered normal in spring.

PRE-RUNOFF TROUT FISHING

Before snowmelt begins, trout streams and even the largest trout rivers tend to run at modest volumes. Many are low and clear. The water is colder than trout and trout fishermen will like it later, but it's warmer than it was in winter. The length of daylight (photoperiod) gets longer with every passing day. Aquatic insects become active, and trout respond and feed on those active insects.

Pre-runoff trout fishing takes place on the edge of winter. Everything you learned in the last chapter about fishing streams in winter can be applied during early spring. Nymphing continues to be good, especially down near the stream bottom. Smaller flies continue to produce better results than large ones.

The big difference between winter and pre-runoff spring is the warm period that occurs after the sun has reached its peak. Before noon, the water warms slowly from the chill of night. A pre-runoff morning might reach the warmth of an earlier winter day when the weather was mild — that magic

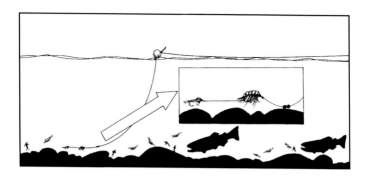

Early-Spring Nymphing — Two-Nymph Rig Fished with Strike Indicator and Split-Shot

45 degrees. Morning is a good time for nymphing the bottom with indicator and shot.

Probe the cold but warming waters with a generic Hare's Ear, Muskrat, Fox Squirrel, or Herl Nymph in #12 to #16. Use a floating line, a long leader, a strike indicator, and whatever weight it takes to get your fly to the bottom. If you fish rivers with populations of salmon-fly nymphs, you'll never find a better time to use a big, black, and ugly nymph as weight to drive your smaller nymph to the bottom.

If your streams lack the large insects, tie a couple of smaller nymphs to your tippet. I often use a #12 olive or gray scud pattern above a #16 generic nymph, especially in tailwaters where weedy currents foster scud populations. Wherever you find even small populations of scuds, trout seem eager to eat them. That's why I like to tumble a scud pattern and a generic pattern on or near the bottom in early spring.

Midges and little olives don't stop hatching just because the weather gets warmer. Their hatches tend to become more intense as the season trots along. These midge and little olive hatches are the most important in winter and continue to be among the most important in early spring.

By far the best dry-fly fishing in pre-runoff conditions is in the afternoon, when the water is warmest. That's usually why I recommend nymphing through the morning, then reining yourself in for a while to watch the water for rises. You'll generally see most activity between one and three o'clock in the afternoon. If you don't focus on trying to detect this activity, it's easy to miss it entirely.

The mayfly hatches of spring are not all olives and not all small. The earliest true spring mayfly hatches include the famous Gordon quills *(Epeorus)* in the East and the slightly less famous march browns *(Rithrogena)* out West. Both are large insects, matched with #12 dry flies.

Nymphs of these larger insects get restless in the morning as the sun slowly warms the water, so larger imitations can provide excellent nymph fishing at that time. Try tumbling a #12 Pheasant Tail or Fox Squirrel in the edge currents alongside fast riffles and runs. The nymphs of both groups are *clingers.* They can stay on stones in the very fastest water. But they migrate into slower water before letting go for the brief swim to the top. Trout hold at the edges of the fast water, so when the natural nymphs migrate across the bottom, trout are there to greet them.

You can take advantage of this by tumbling nymphs along the same edges before a Gordon quill or march brown hatch. Action won't be furious. But you'll see your indicator dip under quite a few times in the couple of mid-morning hours during which this kind of fishing can be effective.

When the actual hatch begins, and this is always in early afternoon, you're sure to have no trouble noticing it. These mayflies emerge on the surface of the edge currents where the water is fairly calm. They also emerge in tailouts above a riffle or run, or in the flats where fast water loses its bounce. Trout that are rising vigorously to take #12 insects on this kind of water are not at all difficult to spot.

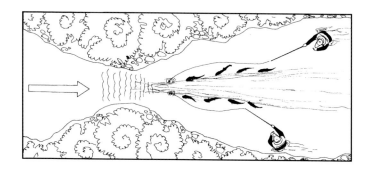

Fishing for Trout Lined Up to Intercept Migrating Clinger Nymphs

I'm not going to give you a grand dissertation on how to fish these hatches. I will tell you that you must match such large insects quite closely with your fly pattern. Don't depend on the traditional principle that a #12 or #14 Gordon Quill will match the eastern species and a #12 or #14 March Brown will match the western types. Take time to capture a specimen early in the hatch and examine it closely.

Most often you'll discover exactly what you expect — a Gordon quill or march brown dun. But the early-season prerunoff period is full of surprises. You can easily discover that you're dealing with one of the smaller sulfurs or pale morning duns. At times, what looks like a march brown at a distance becomes a smaller blue-winged olive when you hold it in front of your nose.

Once you've decided what is hatching and have selected a matching pattern in the right size and color, be sure to refine your tackle to suit the presentation you're about to make. Careful presentation is at least as important as pattern if you're going to fool many trout. Your leader should be tapered to two or three feet of 5X if your fly is a #12 or #14, the same length of 6X if it's smaller than that.

In water where Gordon quills and march browns hatch, you can nearly always present your flies upstream to the trout. Only in the smoothest water of spring creeks and tailwaters are the reach cast and downstream wiggle cast needed to fool fussy trout. These insects do not live in those habitats, so you'll do fine with the upstream presentation.

When making an upstream cast, always remember that your line should not fly through the air over the heads of the trout. That will frighten them. Choose your casting position off to the side, and make your cast at an angle upstream and across the currents to avoid lining the fish.

I'll give you an example of a hatch that nearly defines pre-runoff trout fishing. It takes place in early May on the Yellowstone River in Paradise Valley, just above Livingston, Montana. In most places, May is post-runoff. In Montana that's not always true. Runoff on the Yellowstone River starts on the plateau in the Park at over 7,000 feet, and it starts most years in early May.

Sylvester Nemes, author of *Soft-Hackled Fly Imitations* (published by Nemes, 1991), calls this hatch the *Mother's Day caddis.* "It always happens right around that holiday," Sylvester says. "Not long after, it's over."

Mother's Day caddis are #16 and relatively dark. When they emerge, they appear abruptly in early to mid-afternoon, in bunches. The water is dotted with dozens of them. Sometimes they hatch so heavily that the wind gathers them into rafts against the rocky shoreline.

Trout gather like schooling sharks during the hatch. Their pods tighten until what you see is a compact knot of noses lifting out of the water and falling back, taking caddis. So many naturals speckle the water that you make a frantic cast but then can't determine which dark dot is your fly.

Finally you begin stunning a few of those noses when you creep up close, 15 to 20 feet, and make your casts so short that it's easy to pick out your fly and follow its drift. If you're like me, with this kind of fishing you're pretty happy to be catching browns and cutts and rainbows up to 16 inches long on dry flies when the snow is still flying, even if it is supposed to be spring.

It will be spring on the river in an instant. Temperatures that prompt this hatch also cause snow to begin melting in the Park. Runoff begins with a bang on the Yellowstone. One day you fish the river and enjoy what you're sure will be the best fishing of the year. You just might be right. The next day you drive eagerly out, park your rig, and stride to the center of Carter's Bridge to scan the water for rises. You look down and are dismayed to behold a sea of tan silt. The river is out. It will be for weeks.

Pre-runoff fishing is all over.

SPRING OPPORTUNITIES IN SPATE

High and dirty water, whether caused by snowmelt or rainstorms, is considered the normal spring condition on many rivers. But recall the option to find a place where it's not. For example, when runoff blows the Yellowstone out, it's only an hour's drive to the lower Madison River, which will be in shape because of the dam upstream at Ennis. The Mother's Day caddis hatch will just be getting started there.

You won't always have the option of going elsewhere and will have to fish full water or not fish at all. That's okay. You can still hope for a few trout.

The first thing you should do is check the clarity of the water. Wade in, look down, and see how deep you can still see your toes. That's about the range at which a trout will be able to see your fly. If it's only a couple of inches, I suspect you can find a better way to spend your day. If water clarity extends to as much as half a foot to a full foot, stick around, do some patient casting. If you can see your wading brogues a couple of feet down, then rig your rod with enthusiasm.

A caution: high water means tough wading. The current will be pushy. You won't be able to see the bottom to watch where you're stepping. The water will be cold; you don't want to fall in. Carry a wading staff and use it as a third leg. Probe the bottom with it. Always keep one foot planted while the other explores for its next place to land.

Wear neoprene waders during runoff. They're warm and they also offer some flotation. If you fall in, they lift you like a life preserver. But that same lift can cause problems when you're wading; the current has a broader surface to push against so the neoprenes tend to lift you slightly as you wade. It's more difficult to plant your feet. Wear neoprenes, but wade carefully in them. End of caution.

Reading water to find fish is a critical skill during runoff, for two reasons. First, heavier water reduces the number of lies where trout can escape the current. Second, trout are unable to see your fly at a distance. If you pinpoint potential lies, you can cast to precisely the right spots. You'll launch some trout into the air out of all that somewhat silty water.

The current and the places trout can escape it are your keys to reading water. Look for boulders, but remember that not all of them break the surface. Many will be submerged, sending boils up to the surface, a clear indication that there is a holding lie down below.

A lot of the best runoff water gives few hints about these lies. How do you tell if a featureless run or pool holds some trout? Look at the landscape around you. If the banks are tumbled with stones and rocks basketball-size and bigger, it's a good bet that the bottom is punctuated with potential lies. Fish such water with disciplined casting, showing your fly to all possible lies, and you'll probably stir up some action.

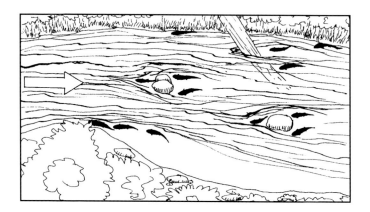

Trout Lies in High Water

If the banks are sandy or silty, it's likely the bottom will be the same. Move on to a bouldered run, a corner, or a pool that has a few big rocks lying along its banks. When runoff has your stream or river high and cloudy, don't waste much time fishing water that looks like it lacks trout.

Trout nearly always hold on or near the bottom during runoff. You must fish deep. If you normally cast five feet above a lie to give your fly time to sink, during runoff you might have to cast 10 to 15 feet upstream to deliver your fly to the same depth. It's wise to use a fairly large fly, one that trout can easily see. It's mandatory to pass that fly through the trout's window of visibility slowly.

Nymphing is the most effective method during spring runoff. Your flies should be #8 to #12. I don't know precisely why brass-bead eyes are so attractive to trout, but adding them to your nymph pattern will double or triple its effectiveness in opaque water.

If you've never fished bead eyes before, in any season, here's a suggestion: *when nothing else is indicated, try a bead-eye nymph in a size that complements the condition of the water.*

Bead-Eye Nymph

If it's low and clear, use a #16. If it's a little swollen, use a #14. If it's tinged with silt, try a #10 or #12. If the water is high and cloudy, use a #8.

Always fish nymphs deep during runoff. You'll need extra weight to get them down; it's smart to tie a couple of nymphs on your leader if local law allows it. You'll need a long leader, 10 to 12 feet. Fix the indicator near the line tip. Make it a large one; it's going to have to suspend a lot of weight without getting pulled under.

If you're ever going to use stout gear, runoff season is the perfect time to do it. Trot out your 7 or even 8-weight outfit. Use a 9 to 9 1/2-foot rod to loft lots of line off the water. A slow rod will keep you from casting constant tangles. A hint: if you own a fast #6 or #7 rod, arm it with a double-taper line one size heavier than the rod manufacturer's specification, or a weight-forward line two sizes heavier. Either will slow the rod action down and let you make the mandatory short casts with an open line loop and therefore lots fewer tangles.

Nymphing techniques do not change a lot during runoff. You still cast upstream and fish back downstream. A free drift of the indicator still offers the best clue that you're getting a good drift along the bottom. But you do need to make two variations to your technique at this time. First, it's better to spend most of your time casting to the best looking lies rather than covering all of the water at random. Second, your casting discipline over those lies should be greater than it is when the water is clear and trout can see your fly a lot farther.

When nymphing during spring runoff, place each cast a mere six to 12 inches from the cast before. The fly should paint a parallel brushstroke on the bottom just inches from the one painted by the previous cast. This is critical. You must show the fly to every single slice of bottom in a potential holding lie. Then your indicator will begin to dip down, and you'll lift your rod to goose an occasional trout into the air, your nymph pinned in its lip.

Streamer fishing is the traditional way to take trout during runoff. It works, but I think it's less successful than nymphing.

The biggest mistake most folks make during high water is to fish a streamer on a long leader and floating line, the same way they'd rig in summer or fall. They fish it on the swing, on a tight line, and expect it magically to sink, simply because it's a streamer and streamers are supposed to sink. But in high water it won't, and trout won't rise up very far to rap it.

It's most effective to fish streamers very slowly on the bottom during runoff, the same way you fish nymphs. It takes different rigging to do it. You still want that stout rod, but get rid of the floating line. On small streams, use a 10-foot sinking-tip. On medium-sized streams, use a 20-foot wet-belly. On large rivers, use a 30-foot fast-sinking wet-head line. Shorten the leader to four or five feet of 2X or 3X. It must turn over heavy flies and be able to handle heavy fish.

Choose a streamer large enough to show in the water you're fishing and weighted enough to get to the bottom of the stream. Usually you'll want a sculpin pattern, such as the Spuddler or Muddler, or an olive or black Woolly Bugger. Use #10 or #12 flies on small water, #6 or #8 for average streams enlarged by runoff. Select #2 or #4 flies on large rivers and

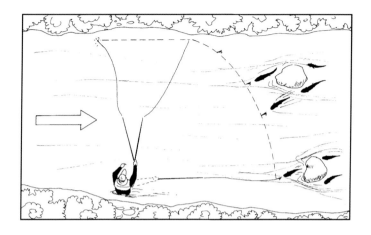

Fishing a Streamer in High Water

for large trout. Any streamer should be weighted with lead wire in proportion to the length and diameter of its hook shank. When you choose the right size fly for the water, you've automatically chosen the right amount of weight to get that fly to the bottom.

Read the water carefully and approach likely lies from upstream or off to the side rather than downstream. This is a great advantage in streamer fishing: you're wading downstream with the current, not upstream against it as you do in nymph fishing.

Don't cast downstream and across. The current will catch the line and hold the fly high in the water. Instead of casting straight across, cast as far upstream as it takes to get the fly to the bottom. Make mends while the fly sinks. Toss slack out behind the sinking head of the line, letting the line draw the fly deeper. When your fly has achieved the depth you want, let the line come tight, and tease the fly downstream and across. Keep your rod low, make mends, and feed line into the drift to slow the swing of the streamer.

Be patient when you fish streamers in high water. Coax them through lies repeatedly. Lengthen your cast, or step downstream, just a foot at a time, to show the fly over a slightly different sweep of bottom on each cast. That's all, except you should be warned that the trout you catch this way at this time of year will most likely be big ones.

POST-RUNOFF SPRING FISHING

After runoff is over the fishing year truly opens up. All kinds of opportunities present themselves, from the bottom to the mid-depths and especially up top. Trout lose the grouch they've gotten into when the water was high and cloudy. They follow and gently pluck at foods they are able to see more clearly and take more methodically.

Spring temperatures and less brutal flows spur aquatic insects into activity. A wide variety of insects begin to emerge. Hatches before runoff are usually restricted to the few types we've talked about: little olive, march brown, and Gordon quill mayflies, midges, plus a few early stonefly species. After runoff, many more mayflies and stoneflies, plus a few caddisfly species, become active.

Add a few kinds of terrestrials to this sudden variety of aquatic insects, and it's the best time of the year to fish the *searching dry fly*. This is some of the most enjoyable and productive trout fishing you'll have throughout the year.

Hatches before runoff tend to be condensed and restricted to a single type of insect. Trout get selective. After runoff, when they see such variety, trout become a lot less selective. Don't get me wrong: if a specific hatch occurs in late spring, trout will key on it and you'll need to match it. But fish are more likely to feed opportunistically on post-runoff streams because hatches tend to be spread out, sporadic, and overlapping.

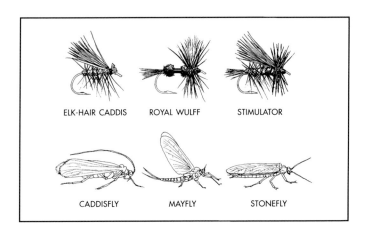

ELK-HAIR CADDIS   ROYAL WULFF   STIMULATOR

CADDISFLY   MAYFLY   STONEFLY

Searching Dry-Fly Patterns

You can coax trout to nearly any dry fly, so long as it looks alive and you present it well, without drag.

Flies that look alive to trout, and that fish well as searching dries, have three things in common. First, they have the shape of one of the primary insect orders: a mayfly, caddisfly, or stonefly. Second, they float well and are heavily hackled to present an illusion of movement to trout viewing them from below. Third, they have bright wings to make them visible to the angler viewing them from above.

The Elk-Hair Caddis, Royal Wulff, and Stimulator are examples of searching dry flies shaped like caddisflies, mayflies, and stoneflies. All float well and look buggy from below. If you use light-colored wings, all are visible from above. Any fly that floats well and that can be seen by the angler from a fair distance can be an excellent searching pattern.

In certain fly-fishing situations, one searching pattern surpasses the others I've mentioned. This is a parachute pattern with moose hair tails, a dubbed brown body, and brown hackle wound thickly around a wingpost of yellow polypro yarn. In spring, lots of water dashes along and generates foam. The yellow wing of this pattern stands out on water dotted with flecks of white foam.

Skip Morris, author of *Fly Tying Made Clear and Simple* (Frank Amato Publications, 1992), showed me how to use this fly on a favorite tiny stream. He cast his yellow-winged parachute upstream onto the small, dark pools, watched it carefully, and set the hook if he saw a splash. To my surprise, and the surprise of quite a few trout, Skip also set the hook a few times when the fly disappeared momentarily.

"A gentle take," Skip said, as he danced a wild cutt toward his hand. "I didn't see it hit. But you sure notice it when that yellow dot suddenly disappears."

It's a common mistake, when fishing attractor dries over post-runoff trout, to select flies a few sizes too large. You read about success with #6 and #8 Royal Wulffs or Stimulators, or #8 and #10 Elk-Hair Caddis patterns. These stories take place on the largest riffles of the biggest brawling western rivers. More often, such large flies fail to draw trout to the surface even on those waters.

On the trout streams that you and I fish most of the time, large flies will draw up only a few little tiddlers. It's easy to think you're doing well because you're catching fish, but that's not true if all the trout are small. Large ones are smarter than small ones. They know the average-sized bites they take up top are the same as the average-sized bites they take down below — rather small.

Try this sometime: if you're using a #10 or #12 attractor dry, and catching few fish or nothing but small ones, drop your dry down to a #14 or even #16. Step up closer and cast shorter. This will help you follow the drift of the fly and will also enable you to make more careful presentations. Try this for yourself and see if you don't suddenly begin catching more and larger trout on the smaller flies.

While we're idling here on the brink of summer, I'd like to enlarge on this idea about smaller flies taking bigger fish. Catch-and-release is responsible for it happening. With that new ethic, trout live longer and grow larger in size. But there's more to it than that. Fishing tiny flies (#16 to #24) gives you an edge on the average guy presenting less realistic #10 and #12 flies. Larry Tullis pointed this out in his brilliant book in the Library, *Fly Fishing for Trout: Volume Three — Small Fly Techniques.*

Tackle for searching dries should be a bit strong. You'll fish a few large flies. You'll want to be able to switch to indicator and shot nymphing if dries fail. My favorite searching rod is 8 1/2 feet long and fishes best with a double-taper floating 5-weight line, though it's rated for a 4-weight. It is snappy and quick. It will easily lift a fly at 40 feet and enable you to drop it lightly back to the water at 50 feet with a single back and forward cast.

A lot of searching fishing is done over broad riffles and runs. It's helpful to have a searching rod that will cast a fairly long distance, at least 60 feet. It's not easy to follow the drift of a dry fly at that range, nor is it easy to detect a take or set the hook. But if 60 feet is as close as you can wade to some sweet-looking, post-runoff holding water, then it would be a shame to walk away from it because you can't reach it. Use a rod that will handle any situation when you're covering lots of water in the spring of the year.

Covering water is essential to searching fishing. If trout were rising, you could spot them and cast precisely to them. When you do have to search the water, you have few indications about exactly where you might find the fish. So you're better off setting up a disciplined casting pattern that shows your fly over all of the potential holding water.

If you find yourself on a small stream, start at the foot of each pool and place careful casts to all likely holding water.

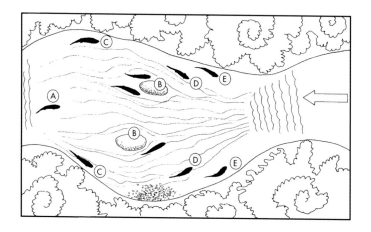

Small-Stream Holding Lies

As shown in the illustration above, hit the tailout (A) and any boulder lies (B), and the bank water (C) if it's deep enough to hold trout. Fish both sides of the current tongue (D) at the head of the pool. Hit the corners (E) where the riffle or run above plunges into the pool.

On a trout stream of average size, you'll fish riffles or runs more often than pools. Show your fly to all potential holding lies. (See illustration on the next page.) Hit the tailout (A), and all boulders (B) with careful casts, both above and below them. Cast over any gravel waters (C). If the bank water (D) is deep, cast so your fly dances right down the edges. Cast to a seam (E) formed by the current so that your fly gets a long drift to one side of it, then down its center, finally on the other side. You never know precisely where trout will find their comfort zone when they are holding under a current seam. But they'll be there somewhere. Before moving on, cast to the corner pocket eddies (F).

Break a big river into its parts and fish each part with searching flies the way you'd fish the same kind of water on a smaller

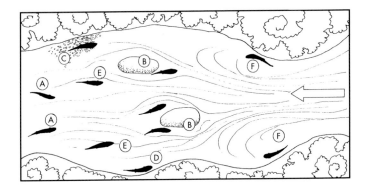

Medium-Sized-Stream Holding Lies

stream. As indicated below, most trout in big rivers hold in broad riffles (A), along the banks (B), on the bottom between center currents (C), on gravel shallows (D), in back eddies (E), or on broad tailouts (F). These are all excellent places to fish with searching dry-fly patterns, provided the water is shallow enough so that trout are willing to rise from the bottom to strike flies on the top. In deeper runs and pools, trout might be present but they might be unwilling to rise all the way to the surface for a dry fly.

Big-River Holding Lies

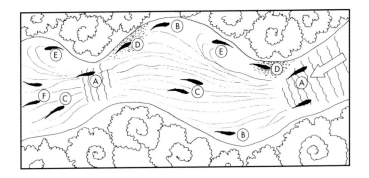

To fish big riffles with dry flies, set up a system that allows you to cover all of the water. Begin at the bottom end of the riffle. Make your first cast straight upstream from your position, no more than 40 feet. Lay the second cast a foot or two to the side of the first. Place the third cast a foot or two to the side of the second cast, and so on. Each subsequent cast should work a foot or two out from the one before it.

When you've searched all of the water you can easily reach from your first casting position, wade into a new position and repeat the entire process. If the riffle is broad and shallow, take up your new position straight out from the first. If the riffle is too deep for you to wade far from shore, move upstream to a point just short of where your first series of casts landed. Cover the next section of water in similar fashion with another series of disciplined casts.

Certain conditions indicate success with searching dry flies. Learn to recognize them. The first indicator is a stream that has dropped and cleared: the essential definition of a post-runoff stream. The second is a warmth in the air, which promises active insects. The third indicator is the visible presence of a few of those insects. The best indicator of all is the sight of sporadic rises, proving trout's willingness to feed on the insects scattered over the surface of the water.

When all these conditions coincide — relatively clear water on a warm spring day, a few insects out and sporadic rises to them — the time is right for fishing the searching dry fly. Try it. You'll be surprised, and so will I, if a few trout don't take your fly.

I'll add a hint here on a tactic that has often worked for me. If trout rush at your searching dries, sometimes splash them, but refuse to take them, switch to soft-hackles or wet flies. Fish them upstream on small streams, or swing them

OVERLEAF: *A spring morning on the Colorado.*

downstream on medium-sized to large water. We tend to denigrate this as mere *chuck-and-chance-it*. But in the spring, nature tosses lots of her natural insects onto the water and lets the current have its way with them. If you cast a wet fly or, even better, a pair of wet flies onto the water and let the current do the same, you'll be imitating a lot more of life than you know about. Trout will applaud, and you'll get to hold them in your hands.

When the water and weather settle down in post-runoff spring, steady insect hatches become more common. If a heavy hatch occurs, it's likely to dominate everything else, and trout get selective. Even if other insects are around, when one particular species of insect suddenly becomes available to trout in overwhelming numbers, trout usually ignore the rest.

To fish a hatch successfully, you need to know precisely which insect the trout might be taking. During the abundance of spring, two or three hatches can occur at the same time. These are called *masking hatches*: a larger insect, say a #12 caddisfly, obscures the presence of a #18 little olive mayfly. This might not seem important, except that, given a choice, trout will ignore the caddis and take only the olives. So if you only glance at the water long enough to see the caddis, then go ahead and match it, you could be in for a long and frustrating day of casting over rising trout without catching any.

I'll give you an example of a masking hatch. I fished the Bighorn River in Montana one late spring, over a pale morning dun hatch. I had the hatch well worked out: I knew it would start in late morning, trickle off most of the day, and keep the trout interested in feeding. I also knew which fly would work — a #16 Pale Morning Comparadun.

One day, after successfully fishing the Comparadun on pod after pod of trout all down the river, I ran into a group of snotty fish that would have nothing to do with it. PMDs drifted down to the fish. Large snouts rose right in the middle of them.

I cast as carefully as I could at first, presenting that fly right down their feeding lanes. Nothing happened. I began casting faster and faster, spurred on by that slight panic that sets in whenever I can't figure out what to do. Still nothing happened.

I finally stopped casting, lifted my binoculars, and scanned the water carefully. I felt like a fool: a flotilla of #20 olives was easy to see, floating along among the larger PMDs. I followed the drift of dun after tiny dun down to death. No snout ever rose to take a PMD.

I added three feet of 7X-tippet, tied on a #20 Little Olive Comparadun, cast it out, and within minutes set the hook into one of those nibbling noses. The trout took off downstream, shot into the air, landed on a straight leader, and broke the fragile tippet. I babied the next fish and was able to lead it into my landing net. It was a brown, more than 20 inches long: one of the small ones in that snotty pod.

A masking hatch is the first thing you want to look for when fishing a steady rise in post-runoff spring conditions. The second thing you should focus on is the life-cycle stage of the particular insect that the trout are taking.

Mayflies, the most condensed and consistent of spring hatches, leave the bottom as nymphs, struggle out of the nymphal shuck at the surface, and drift a few moments as duns before flying away when their wings are dry. Trout feed on ascending nymphs, struggling emergers, or floating duns. All you ever see are the duns and the rises of the trout.

It's difficult to tell which stage the trout take. Yet most trout concentrate on one stage and ignore the others. One trout will devour duns while the one next to it delights in the emerger in the film or the nymph as it nears the surface. How do you tell these insect life-cycle stages apart?

First, if any duns go down in rises, it's obvious trout are taking duns. Second, if a bubble is left in the rise ring but no dun goes down, chances are the trout took an emerger in the

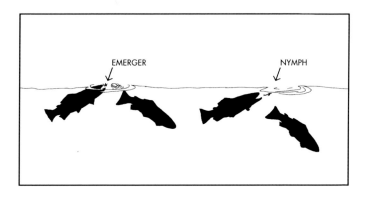

Reading Rise Forms

surface film. This is because a bit of air is taken down with the insect, then escapes as the trout submerges. The bubble of air rises and resides in the rise ring. Third, if you see a rise, but no dun disappears and no bubble is left on the surface, you can surmise that an ascending nymph got intercepted just beneath the water's surface.

Not every situation is this well defined and easy to read. But often enough, if you watch fish feeding on mayflies, you'll notice that some take duns, others take emergers, and a few feed on nymphs as they near the surface.

Now that you've figured out which insect the trout are taking and the stage of that insect, it's time to match the hatch with the right fly.

You can match hatches by using slight size and color variations of a few pattern styles. Since most spring hatches are mayflies, let's look at them. Within the order — and this is true for caddisflies and stoneflies as well — each of the species is the same shape. They vary widely in size and color, but all mayflies have the same upwinged sailboat shape. You can pick a single pattern style to match that shape, then vary its size and color, and you've got all the mayflies matched.

The traditional Catskill-style dry fly is based on the mayfly shape; the pattern has long tails, a slender body, upright wings, and a hackle collar to represent the legs and float the fly. You can tie the Catskill dry in #10 for the largest mayflies, down to #20 for the smallest of them. You can tie it in the Gordon Quill or Light Cahill to match most sulfurs, the Blue-Winged Olive to match most olives, and in the Adams to match grayish mayflies.

You might want to fill in with a few peripheral patterns for hatches on your home waters. But you'll be able to match most mayfly hatches, all over the world, with that slim handful of sulfur, olive, and gray patterns.

The Catskill-style fly fishes best on freestone streams. If you fish smoother spring creeks and tailwaters, the Comparadun style will be better for you. This pattern was originated by Al Caucci and Bob Nastasi and is outlined in their excellent book *Hatches* (Comparahatch Press, 1975). The Comparadun has split tails, a dubbed body, and a wing of deer hair flared in an arc of 160 degrees over the body. It floats well. It is durable. It shows trout a perfect silhouette of the natural mayfly dun, without any hackle to interrupt the outline.

A pattern that is changing prospects everywhere is René Harrop's Hairwing Dun. This style has split hackle-fiber tails, a slender dubbed body, five turns of hackle wound over the thorax and clipped on the bottom, and a wing of deer or elk hair that stands up over the body of the fly precisely as the wing of the natural stands above its back.

Carry along with you the Comparadun pattern or the Hairwing Dun pattern in sizes #12 through #20. Select a pale yellow-olive tie for the sulfurs and pale morning duns, a greenish-olive tie for the blue-winged olives, and a gray tie for darker mayfly duns. You'll be surprised how few mayfly hatches you'll encounter, East or West or in between, that you'll be unable to match with this narrow range of patterns.

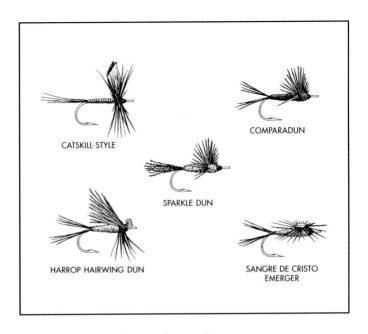

Fly-Pattern Styles for Mayfly Hatches

You should also carry a few patterns that match mayfly emergers. One of the best is the Sparkle Dun. It's a variation of the Comparadun, with Z-lon tails representing the trailing nymphal shuck. Tie it in olive, pale yellow, and gray, in #16 to #20. That will cover most mayfly emerger situations.

Another fly I carry for emergers is the Sangre de Cristo Midge tied in olive or yellow olive rather than black. It's the same fly I use for winter hatches of olives. Not much has changed: I fish it as a dropper off the dry, the dry often serving as an indicator for takes to the emerger.

By matching two stages of the hatch on each cast, you double your chances of discovering which stage the trout are feeding on at the time. But it's difficult to tell which stage an individual trout is interested in unless you can study the trout's rise forms for a while. So it's easier to simply show it both stages. If a few fish show signs of feeding on nymphs, show them a #16 Pheasant Tail on the dropper.

You've solved the first three parts of the hatch-matching problem now: which insect, which stage, and which fly pattern or patterns to match it. All that's left is presentation.

In searching fishing, you make your casts to cover all of the water. When you fish spring hatches, your technique should be just the opposite. First you find rising fish, then you approach them carefully and cast to them precisely.

You hear wondrous arguments between those who think imitation is most important and those who feel presentation is key. Don't listen to either side. Imitation and presentation are two halves of the same thing: fishing a hatch. Get one half right and the other wrong and you're not likely to catch many selective trout. Get them both right and you're going to surprise some trout that have already eluded anglers who foolishly believe imitation or presentation is everything rather than just half of the game.

The most important part of presentation is not casting, but wading into the proper position from which to make the cast. The secret to selecting your best position is to find the closest place you can approach the fish without alarming them, at the same time keeping most conflicting currents behind you. Before wading in, calculate carefully which direction lets you do these two things. Move into position only after you've surveyed the situation.

Once you reach your casting position, consider one of three types of presentation: the *upstream cast*, the *cross-stream reach cast*, or the *downstream wiggle cast*. These three will allow you to cast successfully over rising trout from any direction.

When approaching rising trout from downstream and fishing over them with upstream casts, always remember to cast from slightly off to the side. If you cast straight upstream to a

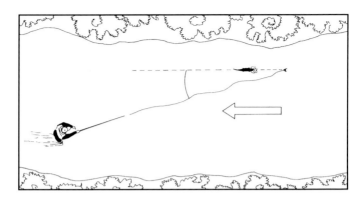

Upstream Cast

trout, the line and leader must sail over it in the air, then settle to the water on top of its head before the fly drifts back down to entice it. By that time the trout is well aware that something foul is afoot. Instead, make your upstream presentations at a 10 or 15-degree angle across the current and you won't warn a trout with your own cast. When your fly arrives in front of it, the feeding trout will be unaware there's an artificial around.

When the best approach requires that you be positioned straight across stream from a rising trout, then you should use the cross-stream reach cast to present your fly. If you instead cast directly across the currents that are flowing between you and the trout, the line will begin to belly and will drag the fly almost instantly. You'll only get a two-foot drift, at most three or four.

To get a longer drift, reach upstream with the rod while the line loop is unfurling in the air. Lean over and reach out as far as you can. The result: the fly will go where you've aimed it, but your line and leader will land at an angle upstream from the fly to the rod tip. Follow the drift of the fly downstream with your rod, and you'll end up with five to 10 feet of drag-free drift, perhaps even more.

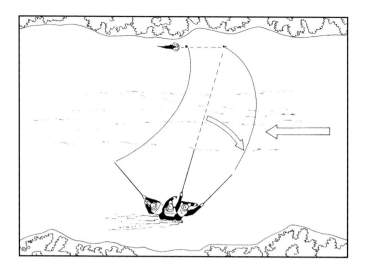

Cross-Stream Reach Cast

To extend the drift even farther, continue to follow the drift of the fly by crossing the rod in front of your body and reaching *downstream.* You'll get drag-free float as long as you can keep the belly of the line from tugging at the fly. This might mean a distance of as much as 20 feet, a lot farther than you'll get when you make your cast straight across the currents. The reach cast also gives the angler the advantage of showing the fly to the fish ahead of the line and leader. It's an excellent way to get chance after chance at a selective trout without alerting it to your presence.

The downstream wiggle cast (illustrated on the next page) allows you to present your fly from a position upstream from the trout. Just as you avoid making a cast from directly downstream, you should never take a position directly above the trout. With the downstream wiggle cast, if the fish fails to take on the first cast, you're forced to pick up for the next cast right on top of the trout's head. That's the end of that.

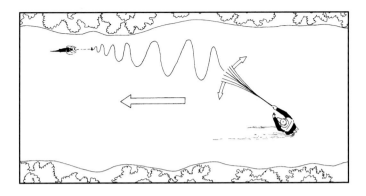

Downstream Wiggle Cast

Instead, take your position upstream but off to the side. Then lay out the cast, aiming the fly two to four feet upstream from the trout and right in its feeding lane. While the cast is still in the air, wiggle the rod gently from side to side. This causes the line and leader to land on the water in a series of curves. As these curves straighten out on the water, the fly drifts freely ahead of them, arriving in front of the fish with no advance warning to the fish.

Remember, the trout will not always be primed to rise the instant your fly gets there. Often you must present your fly over and over until it crosses the magic point at the magic moment. If your first cast scares it, the fish won't be around to see that magic happen. That's why you must be able to lift your fly off the water without making a disturbance, which is why you cast from slightly off to the side. If the fish refuses, let the fly drift past it. Tilt your rod over to draw the line and leader away from the fish. Only after everything is out of the trout's line of vision should you raise your rod and lift the line for the next cast.

These are the three primary approaches to rising trout: the upstream cast, the reach cast, and the downstream wiggle cast.

Combined with the right casting position and the right fly for the stage of the insect you're matching, they'll let you fool lots of trout over mayfly hatches, the dominant spring emergences on moving waters.

SPRING OPPORTUNITIES ON LAKES AND PONDS

Spring turnover is less a reversal of a lake's water column than it is a stirring of the lake's stew. In winter, nutrients in the form of dying plankton settle to the bottom, beyond the reach of sunlight. There they sit, idly decomposing, not prompting the plant growth that prompts insect growth that in turn prompts trout activity.

As soon as the ice goes out, winds set up currents that are not swift but which are of sufficient speed to cycle down to the bottom of all but the deepest lakes. These currents lift and mix settled nutrients throughout the water column of the lake. This phenomenon, called *turnover,* causes lakes to arise to new life in spring.

Sunshine, the energy source for all plant growth, strikes through to the bottom wherever the water is shallow enough. Add the sudden presence of all those nutrients, and you get an awakening of aquatic plants. These form weedbeds that become pastures for aquatic insects, which burst out of their earliest winter instars and quickly grow bigger. They attract trout to the shallows.

So does warmth. You will not be at all surprised to learn that the shallows are the first places in any lake to warm up after ice-out. Add the insects and it's easy to see why the shallows of lakes are the most certain places to find trout in the spring of any year.

The shallows of stillwaters provide an outlet for anglers faced with the spate season on their home streams. But you'd be surprised how few fishermen see stillwaters in this way. They instead do one of two things: continue to fish their streams when it's a fight to do so, or simply quit fishing and wait for runoff to end. Smart anglers take time in spring to have a look at whatever lake fishing might be around.

All this wind about stews getting stirred, insects getting fat, and trout gathering in shallows might sound like a lot of pure theory. How does the theory get put into trouting practice? I'll give you an example.

Some friends and I drove up to Yellowstone Park not long ago. Spring had just arrived, in late June at that elevation, and the ice had just gone off broad Yellowstone Lake. This water looked like our best bet. We slept late the first morning; there's rarely a reason to be on a lake before the sun has had a chance to warm it in early spring.

About ten o'clock we parked at the edge of the lake, not a hundred feet from the main park road. Nothing seemed to be going on, which didn't surprise me as the air was still a bit nippy. Yellowstone that day was about as still as it ever gets. Small wavelets lifted and fell along the shore, but even they had a glassy surface.

I've already mentioned that I carry binoculars to sort out masking hatches and to look for bubbles in rise rings. I also use them to spy on folks who happen to be catching trout when I am not. Sure, I could just hike over and ask them what they're using, but if they're like me, they'd tell a lie. So I use the binoculars for lots of things.

I looked far out onto the lake. Fishermen in boats cast lures, and although it's illegal there, it looked like a few of them dangled baits. Others trolled, watching rods that were bent into arcs. I watched those rods from my distant spy point. If there's any action, throbbing rods reflect it.

No rods danced out on the lake that day. All of those folks made the same mistake. They fished way out where they knew the big ones were, and they probably pitied folks like me who had no more than neoprene waders and had to fish near shore where the fish, as everyone out there knew, are always few and small.

But in spring, the big fish are *not* in deep water. That's a lifeless area. Trout, even big ones, are in the shallows for reasons I've already explained: warmth and food.

So I turned my attention to the water much closer to shore. The surface was empty, calmly lifting and falling in those glassy wavelets. I was about to make a mistake myself and return to the pickup, when a slight darkening of the surface a couple of hundred feet down the shoreline caught my attention. This reflected a weedbed on the bottom, just a few feet down. I raised the binoculars again to have a closer look.

I noticed a scattering of tiny specks. That's all: something afloat but nothing to arouse my interest. Somehow it did, though, as anything out of place on any water rouses the predatory curiosity of any angler, or should. So I hiked a hundred feet closer and raised the binoculars again. Those myriad specks turned out to be mayfly duns. That discovery caused me to scoot right up near the weedbed.

The tiny dimples appearing among the mayflies were barely discernible, even with binoculars. I wasn't sure if I actually saw them or just imagined them. I stared for a long time, still suspecting I saw something moving among the mayflies. Then right in the center of my focused field of vision, a big nose lifted out of the water and sank back out of sight. An insect went down to disaster with it.

That goosed a shout out of me. I ran for the pickup. My friends, not aware of what I'd seen, ran toward it in panic, certain I'd seen a grizzly and was racing for my life. They were wrong. I was racing for my fly rod.

It's not necessary to bore you with the rest of the details of this short story. We strung our rods in the fumbling rush that fishermen get into at the sight of big trout rising. We slipped into waders, high-stepped down to the water, and slid into the shallows.

Two fellows parked their pickup next to ours and watched us fish. They saw us catch quite a few trout, including some that pushed the three-pound mark, as Yellowstone Lake cutts tend to do. They caught our excitement, ran to get a raft, pumped it up, then paddled furiously out past us toward those folks on the horizon who tended untapped rods. That's how sure most anglers are about fishing the depths, not the shallows, of any lake at any time of year.

When I saw that first trout among the duns, I collected a few of those mayflies that hatched in the shallows. They were #12 speckle-wing quills (*Callibaetis*), brown on the back but pale olive on the underside. We matched them with Harrop Hairwing Duns that had dun tails, olive bodies, dun hackles clipped on the bottom, and natural, gray deer-hair wings. The trout were rather selective to this pattern, ignoring the few collar-hackled patterns I tried first.

Your opportunities in lakes in spring are limited to the depth to which sunshine penetrates the water. Why? Because that's the deepest that rooted plant life can grow. The bottom out beyond the point where sunlight strikes even feebly does not push up photosynthetic growth, so look for your fishing in water where you can see the bottom of the lake. I call this the *limits of light*.

The limits of light will be found at different depths in different kinds of lakes. In clear water you'll sometimes see weedbeds at 25 feet. If the water is cloudy, you won't be able to see very far into it. Not surprisingly, sunlight won't penetrate very far into it either, and the bottom might be barren of weedbeds at eight to 10 feet.

This explains why, in a high mountain lake with water clear as air, you can catch fish far out from shore. In a lowland lake

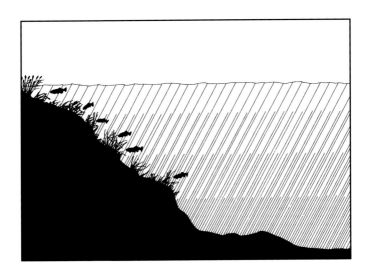

Limits of Light

that is slightly cloudy, the farther you get from shore the fewer fish you catch, because sunlight can't penetrate the cloudy water to reach the bottom very far out unless the entire lake is shallow. The clearer the water, the more scattered its fish are apt to be; the cloudier the water, the more likely trout will be restricted to the shoreline and shallows.

Trout spend most of their time in the shallows in spring because that's where it's warmest and where insects are most active. How do you catch them there? The best way is to find them feeding on some specific food form, match that food form at least roughly with your fly pattern, and present the fly in the way the natural might move.

Spring hatches occurring in the shallows of a lake are primarily those of mayflies, midges, and damselflies. An awareness of each of these types, and a fly box containing a few fly patterns to match them, will greatly increase your fishing success in lakes during the spring of the year.

Mayfly hatches create the most visible activity. Watch the water until you see duns start to pop out and rise rings begin to form among them. Then select a pattern the size, form, and color of the dun, cast it out, let it sit, and set the hook when a trout rises to take it.

When a mayfly hatch unfolds on a stillwater, choose your flies for the duns from the same set of styles used for fishing calm waters on streams. You don't need flotation. Compara-duns and Harrop Hairwing Duns will serve you far better than hackled Catskill-style dun patterns.

Pay careful attention to the color of the insect before you select a pattern color to copy it. I stress this because the back-side of the natural dun is almost always darker than the un-derside, which is what trout observe from a distance of a couple of inches in the instant before a take. In my experi-ence, most spring duns on stillwaters have tan bodies with some shades of olive mixed in and are sized from #12 to #16. That tells you the limited range of fly patterns you need to carry to match most of them.

When casting over trout rising to mayfly duns, present your fly where trout will come along to notice it, rather than cast-ing it constantly into every rise ring that you see. It's tempt-ing to keep casting. A trout rises here; you cast to it. Another trout rises there; you lift the fly and cast to it. Then another trout . . . soon you've put all the trout down. Instead, cast out, let the fly sit awhile, and wait for fish to come and find it.

Fishing a mayfly hatch is simple when they take duns and are willing to accept dry imitations. It's not so simple when they appear to be taking duns but refuse your imitations. When this happens, it's most likely they're feeding on nymphs rising to the surface for emergence.

When trout feed on mayflies, they see the restless nymphs rising from the bottom long before any duns begin to arrive on top. Trout take nymphs first and switch to duns later if

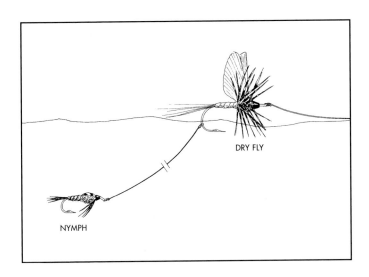

DRY FLY

NYMPH

Dry-Fly and Dropper Rig

the duns become so abundant they're easier to capture. Unfortunately, mayfly hatches on lakes and ponds occur clearly and visibly on top of the water only about half the time.

The other half of the time, fish continue feeding on nymphs even when what you see, and what they seem to be taking, are duns. This half of the equation is difficult to solve until you realize it's happening. Then it becomes easier.

Whenever you have trouble catching trout when duns are out, cease casting and watch the water awhile. You don't need binoculars, although that helps. Follow the careers of a few duns. Do the insects disappear in rises, or rise themselves and fly away? If they are taken, you're on the right trail trying dries. If all those that you watch wing away, then trout are almost certainly feeding on nymphs.

You can tie a nymph pattern as a dropper about two feet behind the dry you're already using. Continue to cast and wait out the rises. This will often solve the problem. Trout will take the nymph soon after it lands, less often after it's been sitting idly for a while. Occasionally move the dry a couple of feet to lift the nymph, and then let it sink again.

Another solution is to nip off the dry and replace it with another nymph. The best pattern I've found is an unweighted Gold-Ribbed Hare's Ear tied 3X long in #12 or #14. The second-best pattern is an olive version of the same fly. Surprisingly, I've had excellent luck fishing spring mayfly hatches on lakes with a winged Hare's Ear wet fly or an olive copy of it, again in #12 and #14.

I fish the nymphs or wets by casting them out, letting them sink awhile, then retrieving them with fairly fast twitches of the rod tip, interspersed with pauses to let the fly sink. Trout take a nymph just as often on the drop, when you can't feel it, as they do on the retrieve, when you can. That's why it's good practice always to straighten your leader before you begin fishing a nymph on a lake or pond. If you have three feet of coils in your leader, a trout can take your fly and run that far with it before you know about it.

Not all trout feeding during a stillwater mayfly hatch take either the duns or the nymphs. Many times they nip instead at a masked hatch of midges. This happens often enough that I've learned to stop fishing and start looking as soon as I fail to catch fish on whatever has been working just moments earlier. I watch the water right next to me, not at a distance. I don't use binoculars for this type of snooping; I want to see what is under the water as well as on top of it.

You rarely see midges on the water, though sometimes you'll see them on the wing. Look instead for cast-off shucks of midge pupae. These are most often tiny, #16 to #20, though a few are larger. They're always difficult to spot.

You can tell the size of the midge pupa from the shuck. But you can't determine its color unless you collect a pupa before the adult emerges. That's a rare thing to have happen but that's why I carry midge-pupa patterns in an array of sizes from #12 down to #20, in a spectrum of colors including black, red, tan, and olive. That covers most midge hatches all across the continent.

To get the color right, you must try one after the other until you find the fly the trout approve. You can try two on the same leader, one dark and one light, or one large and the other small. I generally tie a single midge-pupa pattern as a dropper off the bend of a dry fly, probably the mayfly-dun pattern I was using when I stopped to watch the water for midges. The dropper should be 6X or 7X and at least two feet long. The dry fly serves as a marker, so that when I get a strike on the sunk pupa, I know it. It also suspends the pupa up near the surface and fishes it on the sit. That's the way trout see natural midge pupae: just hanging around, waiting for their time to emerge.

If you fish a midge-pupa pattern by itself, not as a dropper, dress the leader to within a foot of the fly. That will suspend the fly near the surface. Then make your retrieve a creep. Pause now and then to let the fly sit. Most trout will take the pattern during the pause. You might see a slight swirl, but more likely you'll see the leader point jump an inch or two. Set the hook gently. If you're not using a fragile tippet, you're not fishing the midge pupa correctly.

Knowing when to fish damselfly nymphs is a bit more difficult. These are large naturals, #8 and #10. They live in weedbeds, sometimes far out from shore and down near the limits of light, but they must migrate to the shoreline to crawl out for emergence. That usually happens in late spring: May and early June. The migration is what you want to fish. But how do you know when it's going on?

The key is that same watchfulness that lets you know when to fish a mayfly dun, a nymph, or a midge-pupa pattern. Snoop over the side of your boat or float tube. If you see a single

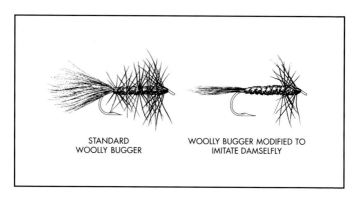

STANDARD
WOOLLY BUGGER

WOOLLY BUGGER MODIFIED TO
IMITATE DAMSELFLY

Modification to the Woolly Bugger

damselfly nymph laboring along, consider it a sign that trout are seeing lots of them making the same journey. Once you've discovered that trout are taking damsels, most of your problems are solved. It's easy to choose a pattern. I use Polly Rosborough's Green Damsel or merely thin the tails and hackles of an olive Woolly Bugger and use that.

Presentation is the key in fishing damselfly patterns. Natural damsels swim with a labored side-to-side undulation of the body. They pause often to rest, sinking slowly as they do. When a trout gets onto their tails, they swim in a burst. You never know in which part of this trip — the idle swim, the pause to rest, or the escape maneuver — trout will intercept the natural. It's best to mimic all three movements.

Rig with a long leader and floating line. On one cast, use a hand-twist retrieve. On the next, retrieve with strips and pauses. On the third cast, retrieve with fast strips to goose the fly right along. Or you can combine all three retrieves on the same cast. Make the cast long. Let the fly settle. Watch your line tip while the fly sinks. Retrieve with a slow hand twist for a few feet. Pause to let the fly settle again. Then strip the fly fast. Repeat the cycle of pause, hand twist, pause, and strip.

Trout will soon let you know which part of the retrieve they prefer. If your experience is like mine, it will nearly always be on the pause. That's why you must fish damselfly-nymph patterns so attentively.

I'll tell you about what I call a *lake intersection,* where a lot of trout hang out in stillwaters in spring. This intersection is the meeting point of three fishing factors: the correct *depth,* the right *fly pattern,* and the best *rate of retrieve.*

The depth of this intersection is the bottom of the shallows, roughly six to 10 feet down. If you can't see trout feeding in spring, assume they're in the shallows but near weedbeds on the bottom. Choose a wet-tip or wet-head fly line that delivers your fly to this depth, and you've solved your first problem in finding spring trout.

Food forms in those weedbeds on the bottom of the lake are almost always some shade of green. If they weren't the approximate color of the vegetation around them, they'd not survive as a species. Choose a fly pattern that is also some shade of green, in #10 or #12, and you're going to interest trout. It's no accident that the olive Woolly Bugger, Olive Hare's Ear, Olive Scud, and Green Damsel are all devastating patterns on trout in lakes.

Your rate of retrieve should be based on the way those food forms move. They creep around in the vegetation or swim slowly near it. Trout are going to take your fly most often if it's green, six to 10 feet deep, and fished with a patient hand-twist retrieve. That's what this lake intersection business is all about. You can catch trout there at almost all times in spring, and even into early summer.

That's what I like about fishing lakes and ponds in spring. Either there's a hatch going on and I'm challenged to match it. Or there's nothing going on and I search idly for that stillwater intersection. Either way, I can nearly always con a few trout into taking one fly or another.

Those trout caught on lakes and ponds in the springtime are more often than not the largest ones I take during the four seasons of the trout fishing year.

SPRING PREPARATION

Spring is defined by the volatility of the weather. I recall a day spent floating and fishing an Oregon river with Richard Bunse and Rick Hafele. When we arrived at the river, we waited at the launch ramp, watching out the car windows while a rainstorm lashed streamside trees. Then the sun burst out, and we eagerly slid the boat into the water.

A mile downstream we were slickered against hail. As we approached the riffles and runs we hoped to fish during an afternoon march brown hatch, the hail softened to snow that swirled briefly around the boat and suddenly stopped. About the time we parked the boat the sun reappeared! A hatch occurred, trout rose, and we were able to hook enough to make us happy to be out there.

You must be prepared for all sorts of weather in a single spring day. You might encounter winter weather, or summer weather, or both. Wear or carry sufficient layers of polypro innerwear and outerwear to keep you warm in the worst of it. A nylon windbreaker is one of the handiest things to have around in spring. It will increase the warmth of whatever layer you find yourself wearing.

You also need a slicker with a hood that will fit over your hat. Carry fingerless gloves. Spring weather can take its toll first on your hands. If they're numb, it's difficult to fish well. In colder regions, I carry a pair of waterproof and insulated gloves large enough to fit over my fingerless gloves.

A caution: if you're float tubing, constant contact with the water can sap heat out of you. Wear neoprene waders and dress more warmly than you think will be necessary. You don't want to risk hypothermia.

It's wise to prepare for the opposite end of the weather spectrum as well. The day just might end up warm and sunny. Then you'll need your lightest layer, just a long-sleeved shirt. Be sure to carry sunscreen. It's likely your nose and ears and cheeks have not seen much sun lately, so you'll be sensitive to sunburn.

Sometime in spring, as the season meanders along and the air slowly warms up, I switch from the neoprene waders of winter to lightweights made of nylon. It's a judgment call when to make this change. Some waters retain the chill of melted snow right up until summer bursts out. In other waters the chill is knocked off in early spring. My rule at this time of year is to carry both neoprenes and lightweights in my ever-present and ever-packed wader bag, which also contains light and heavy polypro underwear. I can then dress and wader myself according to the conditions I find when I arrive at the water I'm about to fish.

Always be prepared to encounter the entire spectrum of conditions, from the heat of summer to the cold of winter, sometimes in the same day. Then you won't have to worry about the weather. You can concentrate on catching those suddenly active and very hungry spring trout.

OVERLEAF: *A hook-up at Sullivan's Slough in Idaho.*

CHAPTER THREE

SUMMER

Summer settles the volatile weather of spring. Creeks, streams, and rivers subside to what we consider ideal size for fly fishing. Stream flows stabilize. In the new warmth of early summer, water levels, insect hatches, and even the behavior of trout all become more predictable.

On average early summer mornings, stream temperatures require time to recover from night's chill, and things are normally slow for a while. Temperatures reach the right levels for insect activity and trout mobility around mid-morning. Fishing gets good then and peaks right in the middle of the day, tapering off in late afternoon and early evening.

Late summer brings on a second set of conditions, often entirely different from early summer. At that time, the water can become too warm during most of the day for much trout activity. Flows diminish. Oxygen levels drop. Trout are least active in the hot middle of the day, most active in the cool hours just after dawn and at dusk and beyond.

Aquatic insect hatches begin to dwindle in late summer. It's not that conditions are poor for hatch activity; rather, most species have already emerged, laid their eggs, and died. If you do get a hatch or a spinner fall, it's likely to occur at dawn or dusk. Fortunately for anglers, terrestrial insects are most abundant — and most active — in summer. Many terrestrials wing their way onto water, or stumble to streamside, where they attract the attention of trout.

These insects rev up their motors and do most of their traveling, whether winging or walking, right through the heat of the day. If stream temperatures remain at a level comfortable for the fish, say below 65 or 70 degrees F., trout will be interested in going after terrestrials or their imitations all day long in both early and late summer.

ANGLING OPPORTUNITIES IN EARLY SUMMER

At the end of spring, water levels recede enough so that you can wade most streams and rivers with ease. Although flows are reduced, water and air temperatures remain at optimal levels for activity of both insects and trout.

In spring, life quickened but tended to be erratic because of the volatile weather. In early summer, life settles into solid rhythms. It's another reason summer is a favorite part of the fishing year: you can fairly well predict what will happen during a fishing day.

Easy wading and predictable fishing are great. The best thing about early summer, however, is the long daily duration of hatches and the wide daily variety of them. Some sort of insect will be out and about all day long, keeping trout alert and feeding on the surface. Often two or three food forms will be busy: one emerging, another laying eggs, perhaps a third tumbling in from shore.

That kind of variety can mean excellent dry-fly fishing. Not only are trout kept alert for food on the surface; they're also less likely to be selective. If they see two or three insect types somewhat sporadically, they're not going to turn up their noses at something that looks a little like any one of them, or even something that just looks like it might be good to eat. When they're not selective to a single food form, trout are apt to try anything that looks buggy.

That's why searching dry flies work so well in early summer, as they did in late spring. It's the prime time of year for them. This is a continuation of the same set of conditions that began to emerge in post-runoff spring: clear water, warm air, a scattering of insects active, a few fish rising to take them.

Most folks think of searching dry flies as #10 and #12 Royal Wulffs, Trudes, and other attractors with flagging white wings. Those are okay on rough riffles and in the pocket water of cascades, where trout don't get much chance to scope out a fly. On those waters you want to use flies that float well and that stand up so you can see them easily.

Few folks think of searching flies as anything smaller. But recall that lecture Rick Hafele gave me about the average-sized nymphs and larvae eaten by trout in winter — around #16. The insects trout take in summer on the surface emerge from those same nymphs and larvae you imitated with nymphs in winter. Sure, they've grown a couple of sizes before emerging. But they've also lost a size or so when they cast off their immature exoskeletons. So they're not much bigger as adults than they were as nymphs and larvae.

The average-sized bite a trout splashes off the surface in early summer is around #14. If trout show a willingness to take #10 and #12 searching dries — which are what you can see most easily on the water — then use them. Most of the time, it's better to reduce the size of your searching dry flies to the smallest you can see on the water you're fishing. I'll give you an example:

I fished the Frying Pan River in Colorado this summer with John Geirach, author of that string of bright books that began with *Trout Bum* (Pruett, 1986). John led me to a narrow side channel that was about 15 feet wide, almost a hundred feet long, and very fast. He pointed up the channel to some brush overhanging its edges. "There are usually a few trout hanging under the brush along the bank up there," he said.

"What'll they usually take?" I asked.

"Doesn't matter too much in that kind of water," John told me before hiking off to fish his own piece of the Pan. "Just try a small caddis."

I looked at the channel bouncing briskly over its bottom of clean stones. It appeared to be great holding water. A current tongue shot all the way down the center, but the water was slightly slower on each side. It would be difficult to see anything smaller than a #12 Elk-Hair Caddis on that riffled water, so that's what I called small and tied to my tippet.

I began casting and worked out about 35 feet of line. My first casts were over the deeper water alongside the fast center current. Nothing happened there. I angled subsequent casts in toward the edge a foot at a time, since the rule in fishing fast water is to cover all of it because you never know where a trout might surprise you. None did. Before long I placed a cast up under the brush John had pointed out.

I saw a splash and a fair-sized flank roll out of the water and dive back down in the same instant. I jerked back to set the hook, but all I did was rip the line off the water and blow the fly over my shoulder. That trout was down. I moved upstream 20 feet and began exploring the next section of water between the current tongue and the bank. The cast that placed the fly back beneath John's overhanging brush drew the same result: a trout splashed the fly, and I put it down by jerking the fly out of there.

Never make trout try to tell you the same thing more than twice. A splashy rise is not often a missed strike — it's a last-instant refusal of your fly. What do you do about it? The rule with searching flies is to go smaller, go darker, or go both. As I tied a #16 Elk-Hair Caddis to the tippet, I realized I was following John's earlier advice: "Just try a small caddis."

I had to move in closer and cast 10 feet shorter in order to see the smaller fly on the water. A trout told me almost at once

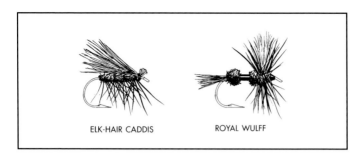

ELK-HAIR CADDIS   ROYAL WULFF

Types of Searching Flies

that John had been right. It expressed its approval of the smaller Elk-Hair by taking it with a satisfied rolling rise that had no splash to it. I took half a dozen more fish before finishing out that side channel. Here was proof of the old cliché: it's sometimes wise to ignore trout-fishing writers, but it's never wise to ignore the trout.

Don't neglect the Royal Wulffs and Trudes and Stimulators that make up the cornerstones of a searching dry-fly box. But be sure to carry them in #14 and #16 as well as #10 and #12. You'll be surprised how many more trout you begin taking with them, especially as the high flows of spring diminish in early summer.

When specific hatches occur in early summer, you must match the hatch just as you did in late winter or in spring. Some of those hatches will continue to be mayflies. But they're less likely to be little olives and more likely to be sulfurs, in the East, or pale morning duns, in the West.

These are both pale yellow insects. Standard ties include the Gordon Quills and Light Cahills, in #12 to #16. These hackled flies are great where the water is slightly rough. However, you'll often run into mayfly hatches on spring creeks and tailwaters, where the water is calmer. In these cases it's best to use more exact imitations.

The same styles that worked for the little olives can be converted in size and color to work well for the sulfurs and PMDs. The Sulfur Comparadun has a pale yellow dyed deer-hair wing flared in a 160-degree arc over the body. The body is a mix of pale yellow and olive fur. The tails are split ginger hackle fibers. To convert this effective pattern to a Sparkle Dun, just substitute tan or clear Z-lon for the tails, to represent the trailing nymphal shuck.

In addition to sulfurs and PMDs, early summer brings hatches of green drake mayflies. These average #12; some are #10. The best pattern I've seen for them is Mike Lawson's extended-body Green Paradrake. It is tied with an olive-dyed elk-hair body, tails of black, moose body hair, and a grizzly hackle dyed green and wound parachute-style around a deer-hair wing post.

Green drakes are big bites. But they're very cranky creatures, especially the western group, in the genus *Ephemerella*. Their hatches are brief, sporadic, and unpredictable. You need to be prepared with a few flies to match them if you hit them. But you're not going to hit them all that often.

You will, however, almost certainly bump up against the smaller blue-winged olives a few times if you get out at all often in early summer. Lots of species contribute to this hatch. One or another of them lives in nearly every trout stream, all across the continent. I won't get into Latin about them, but I will tell you they generally have olive bodies and dun-to-slate wings, and are in sizes #14 and #16.

These can obviously be imitated by the famous and effective hackled Catskill tie, the Blue-Winged Olive. Tie it with blue dun hackle-fiber tails, an olive fur body, blue dun hen-hackle wings, and a blue dun hackle collar. It is most effective in #14 and #16, but you'll also find use for it in #12. Carry it in those sizes and you'll have lots of hatches matched wherever you fish during the early summer season.

Harrop Hairwing Dun

I add another pattern to my fly boxes that covers even more hatches. It's René Harrop's Olive Hairwing Dun in #12 to #20. It is tied with split dun hackle-fiber tails, an olive body, and five turns of dun hackle tucked up under a natural deer-hair wing. The hackle is clipped on the bottom. The wing butts are clipped short to form a head on the fly just like the head of Al Troth's famous Elk-Hair Caddis.

Why do I say that this fly matches so many hatches? Think back a bit: it's the same pattern that I wrote about in the winter and spring chapters as matching little olive hatches. It's the same fly I use on lakes for spring and summer speckle-wing quill hatches, such as those on Yellowstone Lake. Now I've added the green drakes and blue-winged olives to its long list. *Field & Stream* once sent out a questionnaire to its writers. One question was: What fly would you choose if you could carry only one? I had no trouble answering the Olive Harrop Hairwing Dun. Tug it under and you can fish it as a wet fly. Nip off its wings and it's a generic green nymph you'll have trouble improving upon.

Add René Harrop's PMD Hairwing Dun to your fly box in #12 to #18. You'll then be prepared to cover all of the sulfur, PMD, and pale evening dun hatches you might run into, not just in early summer but in spring and fall as well. And you're armed with only two flies in a range of sizes.

Early summer is a transitional time, when caddisflies slowly take over from mayflies to become the dominant trout-stream insect. Caddis are the source of some of the best trout fishing of any season. They're not always easy to notice. When you begin to be aware of them, however, you gain a lot of extra chances for coaxing trout to your flies.

Caddis spend most of their lives as worm-like larvae. Some are cased, others are not. The abundance of caddis larvae is the reason you'll rarely go wrong rolling a #12 or #14 Tan or Green Rockworm along the bottom of a fast, rocky riffle. Use the strike indicator and split-shot technique to fish these nymphs; in faster water you must use more weight than you do when nymphing in slow water.

You can easily decide which caddis-larva imitation to use, tan or green, by hoisting rocks off the bottom of the stream and examining them closely. Be sure to watch awhile; caddis worms don't become active until they've been out of the water at least a minute or two. Then you'll see them suddenly begin hiking around.

It's more difficult to bring the second stage of the caddis, the pupa, under observation. A larva encases itself along the bottom, then transforms into a pupa inside its sealed chamber. Once mature inside the case, the pupa cuts its way out with scissor-like mandibles, then is buoyed to the surface by gases trapped under its skin. It assists its lift with a swimming motion that is sometimes brisk, other times feeble. Either way, the progress of caddis pupae toward the surface is often interrupted by hungry trout.

Caddis pupae are the easiest stage of the insect for trout to observe and eat but the most difficult stage for the fly fisherman to observe and match. It's a brief transition. After leaving the pupal chamber, the pupae float or swim just two to six feet to the surface, then emerge as adults and fire off toward streamside brush like cannon shots.

Fishing Soft-Hackles during Caddis Activity

What you see from your elevated position above the water are a few splashy rises and a few adult caddis flying in the air. You match them with a dry fly but catch nothing. But what trout see from their point of view beneath the water are lots of caddis pupae angling up toward the surface, legs, antennae, and wing cases all trailing and trembling in the currents. That's the stage the trout take, sometimes in such a rush and so near the top that they make a splash. You see the splash, assume an adult died in it, and tie on a dry fly.

Here's the true solution: tie on a soft-hackled wet fly the size and color of the adult in the air. The underwater stage of the caddis will not always be the same size and color as the adult, but it's a good place to start.

I've not found it necessary all that often to collect samples of the pupal caddis. Usually a switch in the level fished, from surface to sunk, is enough to turn the trick. If it's not, then I run through a brief list of soft-hackles, from the Partridge & Green to the Partridge & Orange, Partridge & Yellow, and the March Brown Spider. Pattern recipes for all of these are given in Sylvester Nemes' classic book, *The Soft-Hackled Fly,* which

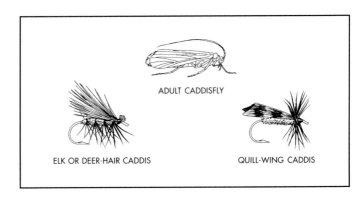

ADULT CADDISFLY

ELK OR DEER-HAIR CADDIS

QUILL-WING CADDIS

Adult Caddisfly Imitations

has been reprinted and is available from Stackpole Books (1-800-READ NOW).

Fish the soft-hackle on a down-and-across-stream swing, right through rises. Use constant mends to slow the drift of the fly. If it's racing, trout will ignore it. When fishing soft-hackles and wets on the swing, let trout set the hook themselves.

I don't want to downplay early summer dry-fly possibilities when adult caddis are out. Some species deposit their eggs in bright sunshine, out over the choppy water of riffles and runs. Others deposit their eggs on smoother water, usually in the calm of early evening. Watch carefully for these events. Neither is easy to notice, one because the water is rough, the other because light is failing.

In either case, try to capture an adult in your hand or your hat, or an aquarium net if you have one. Select an Elk-Hair Caddis in the same size if the insect is tan, or a darker Deer-Hair Caddis tied in the same style if the natural is gray. One of these two patterns will match most caddis hatches on moving water. If it doesn't, then choose a more imitative Quill-Wing Caddis in the appropriate size and color, usually tan, brown, or gray. Most trout-stream caddis come in #12 to #16.

You'd be wise to carry the Elk-Hair Caddis, Deer-Hair Caddis, and a narrow array of Quill-Wing Caddis in #12 to #16. Those few flies handle a lot of caddis situations, on this continent or any other.

But they won't handle them all. Trout-stream caddis seem crazy. They flit through the air erratically and smack themselves into the water like aerial acrobats on kamikaze missions. These caddis are diving through the water's surface to swim down and deposit their eggs on the bottom. That should tell you something about how to fish caddis.

Think back on such situations that you've seen yourself: erratic caddis on the wing, fish feeding in scattered fashion, once in a while a trout tosses itself into the air after an insect. Were any of those bold fish big ones? If so, I've missed them. They're always little tiddlers. The ones you want to catch are down below, feeding on caddis that are swimming toward the bottom to lay their eggs or returning to the surface after completing that mission.

Imitate these diving caddis with wet flies, not dries. That's why I suggested just a bit ago that you select your soft-hackle based on the size and color of the adult insect you see flying in the air. Sometimes trout are after pupae, and the fly you've selected is not a perfect match but still might work. Just as often, however, trout are feeding on egg-laying adults, and the wet fly suddenly fools fish in a situation where dry flies failed miserably.

When you know the situation calls for a match of the diving adult caddis, you're better off fishing an old-fashioned winged wet fly rather than a soft-hackle. Nearly all trout-stream caddis species that exhibit this diving behavior are either tannish-bodied with light brown wings or dark green-bodied with gray wings.

You can match these with a winged Hare's Ear wet for the brownish types and a Leadwing Coachman for the gray types, in sizes #12 and #14. Fish them on the downstream swing, through any rises, or by searching the water with them if adult caddisflies are in the air but you see no fish working on the surface. It's likely they're feeding just beneath it.

That's pretty simple strategy, and the two wet flies are a light load to carry for the number of situations they handle.

These two bits of caddis behavior — the elusive pupa rising toward the surface and the erratic adult diving down toward the bottom — are what convert caddis into such mysteries. Think soft-hackles and winged wet flies when you see caddis in the air but you aren't bringing trout to dries, and you'll nearly always find a solution to their hatches.

Always try dry flies first, however, when caddis are on the wing. If trout are satisfied to take them, you should be more than satisfied to fish them. But I'd hate to have had subtracted from my days those on which I'd been able to turn dry-fly frustration into wet-fly pleasure through knowledge of early summer caddis antics.

Gearing up takes a slight switch at this time of year. In spring, you fished light tackle over hatches, or stout gear with heavy nymphs and streamers. In early summer you'll need to change abruptly from bushy searching dries to hatch-matching dries and emergers, to wet flies, and even to some bottom-thumping nymphs. Obviously you want gear that is versatile, or you'll limit your own chances.

The best sort of outfit for early-summer trouting is an all-around rod, 8 1/2 to 9 feet long, balanced to a 5-weight double-taper line, a 6-weight if you fish big rivers in windy country, such as the Rocky Mountain West.

My own all-around rod is an 8 1/2-foot Cairnton designed by Russ Peak and Kerry Burkheimer. It's rated for a 4-weight line but works better for me when it's loaded with a 5-weight double-taper. When I've got this rod in my hands, I know I'll be able to handle any situation that early summer offers.

Early summer and late summer are divided as neatly as two separate seasons, usually by a sudden spell of hot days. Conditions change dramatically on most moving waters. You must change with them, or you'll find your success dwindling like the midday mayfly hatches.

Hot weather brings about several changes that alter the behavior of trout. Water flows become shallow and slow. Water temperatures warm toward the limit of trout tolerances, just above 70 degrees F., until trout become distressed during midday heat. Warm water holds less oxygen than cold water, so trout become lethargic at midday.

It's difficult to tell which is worse for fish: low water, high temperatures, or too little oxygen. But it's not difficult to determine the cumulative result of all three factors: trout shift their activity out of the center of the day toward times when the water is cooler and contains more oxygen. That means dawn and dusk.

Some mid-summer streams remain cool throughout this season because of their altitude or because they have a steady source of cooling flows. Then a simple switch from fishing in sunshine to fishing in shade makes the difference between boredom and happy quarrels with trout. Sometimes trout gang up in pools that are in shade.

I recall fishing Montana's Smith River with my brother Gene one summer. We explored the length of a hundred-yard-long riffle, all exposed to the sun, without setting the hook into a single fish. Then my downstream progress took me beneath the canopied branches of a tall cottonwood tree. It looked like I'd come across some good water: the riffle dropped over a ledge and into a trench about 20 feet long, 15 feet wide, all in the shade beneath that tree. I'd fished similar lies all down the riffle, but none in such cooling darkness.

I had a pair of wet-fly patterns tied to my leader already, so that I could better explore that long riffle. I cast the two wets just above the ledge and let the current tumble them into the trench. They entered shade and deep water at the same moment. I felt three successive jerks on my line. The first was a trout taking one of the wets. The second was another trout chasing down the trailing fly. The third jerk was the jolt of my leader parting when the two heavy trout took off in opposite directions.

I called Gene, and he waded over while I re-rigged. We surrounded that shaded pool, and it entertained us for about an hour before we exhausted its possibilities. It seems that all the trout from the entire length of the riffle were gathered up in there. We must have hooked, handled, and released close to a dozen trout apiece.

On forested streams, it's only necessary to fish the edges to find yourself in the shade of lofted branches. On some desert streams and meadow streams, trees tend to be more scattered along the banks, and while this puts good lies farther apart, it does make them easier to spot. It also increases their magnetic powers on trout.

I fished a small desert stream this August. Vegetation was sparse on the hillsides above the streambed, but scattered trees grew in the watercourse itself. These cast intermittent shade over the water. One pool would be struck by the sun; the next would be in shade. Because I'm a slow learner, it took me about 10 pools to figure out that the trout were all in shaded pools and never anywhere else.

This kind of information can appear slightly esoteric. It seems that if you just fish all of the water anyway, you'll catch the same number of fish. This is not so. Eliminate pools struck by sunshine and therefore unproductive, and you will double your fishing time spent on water with potential. The same applies to the time fished: if trout are simply not willing to feed in the hottest part of the day, you'll more than double your chances if you quit fishing then and shift your effort to dawn and dusk.

Think how dawn and dusk work to solve those three problems I mentioned earlier: low flows, high heat, and too little oxygen in the water. First, flows in summer are thin and slow, so trout are exposed to predation when the light is bright. Early and late, however, they're less visible, less fearful, and more apt to be active, thus increasing your chances of catching them. Second, at midday, water temperatures approach stressful levels. At dawn and dusk, however, the water is cooler, and trout prowl. Third, when the water is warmest, it also entrains the least oxygen. In the morning and evening, you'll find trout on the hunt for food.

Hatches, though they've tapered off at this late season, also shift from the middle of the day to morning and evening. I fished Silver Creek in Idaho this summer with Jim Hill, a resident who knows not only the river but also its hatches. He delivered me to his favorite piece of the meandering spring creek, sat me down, and handed me a box of flies, an unusual bit of hospitality.

"You might not have what you need," Jim said. "If you don't, you'll find it in there. The Tricos will start in about 45 minutes. I like the white-winged no-hackle." With that advice, he trotted off downstream to his own bit of fishing.

It was a little after 8:00 in the morning. Forty-five minutes would be about 9:00. I sat in the grass, strung my rod, dressed my line, lengthened my leader. I peered into Jim's magical fly box and attached the fly he'd recommended: a #20 no-hackle tied by the great René Harrop himself and featuring a black body and fragile white quill wings. I don't tie no-hackles myself, because mine are less likely to please trout than they are to startle them. Also, they don't last long before their wings become tattered. I was about to discover that shredded wings would not bother the trout during that morning Trico hatch in late summer on Silver Creek.

After all my gear was properly assembled, I inserted myself into a float tube, slipped through a belt of cattails, and slid quietly into the water. I flippered to the nearest open water in the dense weedbeds that nearly choke Silver Creek in summer. That open water was a pinched channel just six feet wide, stretching upstream and down for 200 feet.

It was a wonderful place to be. I'd have been satisfied just to sit and gaze at all the beauty around me. But a tiny reflection over the cattail tops caught my attention, then another and another. It was the glint of sunshine on Trico spinner wings. An ever-increasing ball of insects grew over the cattails, then slowly shifted over the channel and descended towards it, dancing.

The first trout came up not long after. I glanced at my watch. Jim was way off; the spinner fall was 10 minutes sooner than he'd said.

That first trout rose closer than I liked, not much more than a long leader length away from me in my float tube. Sometimes that can be the most difficult kind of cast to make. I waited until the trout rose in a steady rhythm, then I flipped a cast out in the instant after the trout rose and tipped down again. I hoped its focus would be on where it was headed, toward the bottom, rather than where my fly landed, up top.

I don't know if I got that right, but the fly sat on the surface for a long moment, then disappeared in a gentle swirl.

Successfully hooking a trout in a situation like that is plenty of victory for me. I don't need to land it, though I'd never deny the satisfaction of that. I just don't expect it to happen. This trout, stung by the tiny fly in its lip, burned straight down the narrow channel. My backing knot was past the rod tip before the trout put on its brakes and shot into the air. After seeing its size, I was even more certain I'd lose it.

The trout reversed field and made its next run right back up the channel past me. I couldn't reel fast enough to keep up. The line going out and the line coming back were so near each other in the six-foot channel that I'd think I was Lefty if I could cast a loop that tight. I can't, and the trout kept going, drawing that loop out into a cast almost as far upstream as it had gone down, still straight up the pinched channel.

All the trout had to do was swim three feet in either direction into the weeds and it was gone. Crazily enough, it wore itself out racing up and down the channel, then let itself get backed into my landing net. I scooped it up, used the nine-inch span of my hand to estimate it quickly at something over 18 inches, then unpinned that tiny and tattered fly from its lip. I tipped the trout out of the net and watched it ghost away instantly into the weeds.

A moment later, another trout nearly the same size took the fly and fought the same fight.

The spinner fall ended when the day began to get hot, around 11:00. By then I'd hooked eight fish, landed six of them against the odds of that narrow channel, and still had what little was left of that Trico no-hackle Jim Hill had loaned me.

In late summer it's usually mayflies that hatch or fall as spinners early in the morning. It's almost always caddis that hatch or return to the water to lay their eggs later in the day.

I was on the Deschutes River in August when little made sense but to lie in the shade like any smart trout. I didn't become that smart myself until I'd fought the heat for a few fishless hours at midday. Then I sat beneath an alder tree next to the river that is broad and brawling even in the middle of summer. Soon I was snoozing.

I must have slept a couple of hours because I woke up out in the sun. The shade had shifted. The cool of evening had descended, and clouds of caddis had arisen. They swirled in the air. They formed halos around juniper and sagebrush tops, the caddis backlit by the setting sun. More important to trout and to me, they flitted in short sorties from streamside grasses out over the water. I began to see rises right at the edges. This is something you should be aware of at any time of year, not just in late summer: all it takes to cause a little trout activity is a little insect activity.

I slipped to the edge of the river and watched awhile. The rises were splashy. The fish were after the adult caddis. I knew this because I saw a couple of caddis hit the water, float a foot or two, and go down in bold boils. Unlike lots of caddis moments, the situation called for a dry fly, not a wet.

It's not always easy to catch a flying caddis out of the air to get a model for fly selection. It is, however, very easy to thrash the vegetation with your hat and peer into it to see what you've captured. That's what I did. A dozen dazed specimens from two or three separate species crawled around in confusion. They averaged about #14, in light tan. I tied on an Elk-Hair Caddis, rarely a mistake when caddis are on the wing and trout are feeding sporadically on the surface.

The rest of the evening was easy, and I don't want to bore you with the details. All I did was work along the banks of the river, casting that Elk-Hair dry upstream tight against the grasses, where those caddis sorties originated. I didn't catch a lot of trout before it became too dark to fish, just 10 or so. They were not large; none were over four pounds, though several were at least three. And I was a little disappointed that only one agitated rattlesnake wagged its tail at me that entire Deschutes evening.

Mayfly and caddis hatches move to opposite ends of the day in late summer. They also taper off somewhat, simply because most individual insects have already hatched, sowed their seeds, and died. Fewer mayflies and caddisflies are left for trout to feed upon. But trout don't stop feeding. Instead, they turn their attention to terrestrial insects.

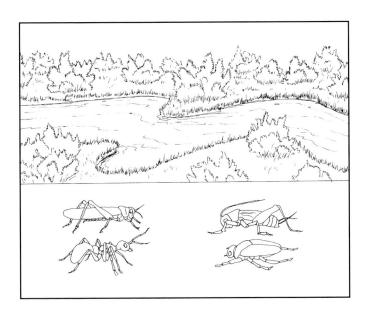

Meadow-Stream Terrestrials

Terrestrial insects falling to the water become the dominant food form on many trout streams in late summer. I'd like to give you something to consider when you think about terrestrials: the wider the river you fish, the more restricted your opportunities for terrestrial activity; the narrower the stream you creep along, the more often terrestrials are important.

If your waters are wide, terrestrials tumble to the water only along their edges. The broadest sweep of water, out in the center, rarely gets a visit from such insects. If your streams are narrow, however, all of the water will be near enough to the banks to be blessed constantly by whatever the breezes might deliver.

This does not mean that terrestrials lack importance on big rivers. It does mean that they're important on those rivers only at the banks. Fish a hopper in the center of a hundred-yard-

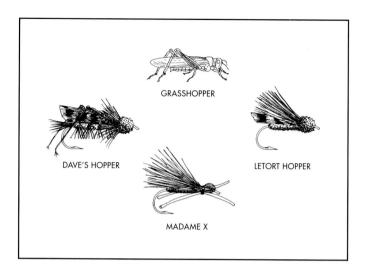

GRASSHOPPER

DAVE'S HOPPER

LETORT HOPPER

MADAME X

Grasshopper and Imitations

wide Madison River riffle, and you're showing it to trout that have not gobbled up a grasshopper in a long time. That's not to say they won't be glad to get it, but it's likely they won't be taking it for a hopper if they do and would be just as glad to get a Royal Wulff or Sofa Pillow.

Toss that same hopper tight to a Madison River bank, however, and trout are likely to take it with the kind of bold boils that indicate they are certain about what they are doing.

Small and medium-sized streams, as well as bank water on big rivers, are the true hotbeds of late-summer terrestrial fishing. Different waters will drop different kinds of creatures to the surface depending on the vegetation beside the water.

Meadow streams such as the Letort and Firehole, or sage-lined rivers such as the Madison and Deschutes, offer up hoppers, crickets, ants, and beetles to their trout.

Tree-lined streams such as the Beaverkill and Pennsylvania's Fishing Creek, or the small willow and alder canopied creeks that we all love to fish wherever we live, are more likely to offer inchworms and termites, as well as beetles and ants.

If grasshoppers are about, they fly out from around your feet when you hike beside a stream. When trout take an errant hopper, they do it with a splash. It's easy to observe the insects, and it's easy to tell when trout take them. If hoppers are present, you should have no trouble telling when it's time to tie one on your tippet. You'll never go wrong using a Letort Hopper, a Dave's Hopper originated by the great Dave Whitlock, or a Madame X.

Crickets are not as widespread as grasshoppers but end up being very important wherever they can be found in abundance and wind up in the water. I've not had a lot of experience with them myself but you can find a wealth of information and advice about them in the newest book on the subject, *Terrestrials,* by the master Ed Koch and his friend Harrison Steeves III (Stackpole Books, 1994). It's a wonderful work on all of these insects and lists pages of patterns for crickets. The most famous is Ed Shenk's Letort Cricket, a black version of his more famous Letort Hopper. Like hopper patterns, cricket imitations are best fished nearer to the banks than they are farther out.

Late-summer weather delivers a lot of other insects to the water, few of them as easy to notice as hoppers and crickets. First among these in importance to the angler are the ants.

When winged ants are out on their summer dispersal flights, you'll have no trouble knowing it. They're large, #12 and #14, and they're somewhat troublesome, crawling around in your hair and all over your clothes. Their fragile wings break away easily. Even if you don't see the ants themselves, you'll probably notice glassy elliptical wings that have been discarded by the naturals.

Winged ants are black or dark brown. Their bodies are bulbous in back and front, the two distinct segments separated by a thin center section where the legs originate. Your patterns, whether winged or not, should reflect this distinct segmentation because it's the key characteristic of the ant.

Most folks use floating patterns when winged ants are out. Koch and Steeves, in their new book, have a full section on the history of fishing sinking ant patterns. I find this interesting because I cannot record the number of times I've found a meager supply of ants topside, then caught a trout and discovered it stuffed with ants that have been taken subsurface. I've always found that an old Black Gnat wet, in #12 or #14, is excellent medicine when this happens.

Most often, ants lack wings and arrive on the water by falling to it, not flying to it. In that case, they'll be very difficult to observe. You'll see trout sipping on smooth water, usually right along the banks or just a few feet out, but you'll see no sign of what they're taking. If you're like me, you'll change frantically through your list of dry flies and subsurface nymphs before you wise up, stop fishing, and put your nose down next to the surface of whatever water you're fishing.

Focus on the water from just a foot above it. You'll be amazed at what you see that you would never notice by looking at the water from five feet up in the air. Sometimes it will be a small mayfly spinner or even a tiny adult microcaddis. Most often you'll find the trout are sipping tiny ants suspended in the surface film.

Ants have waxy bodies that repel water. Larger winged ants are heavy enough to sink when they get wet. Most small ants ride gentle currents awash, half in and half out of the surface film. That's why they're so hard for you to see.

The best ant patterns float flush in the surface film, rather than riding on top of it. The McMurray Ant, with its bulbs of balsa wood painted black or brownish red, is a classic example. It has a slight hackle separating its segments, but the hackle is there to represent legs, not to float the fly. The knobby balsa

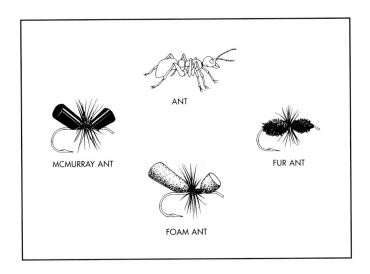

ANT

MCMURRAY ANT

FUR ANT

FOAM ANT

Ant and Imitations

sections float flush, making the fly look just like a natural ant that has fallen to the water.

The Black Fur Ant and Cinnamon Fur Ant should be tied to give the same segmented effect. Dub a knot of fur at the back. Leave a bare section of hook wound with thread and two or three turns of short hackle. Dub another knot of fur at the front. The space between the knots, more than the knots themselves, makes the fly resemble a real ant.

The Foam Ant follows the same principle. Lay the black or red-brown foam over the hook shank and wind enough thread over its center to separate the segments which then rise at either end. Take a few turns of hackle at the center. That's it. No fly will be easier to tie. But no fly will have greater potential for taking trout than a well-tied ant pattern.

All of these ants should be tied in #14 through #20, in two colors: black and reddish brown. If you carry those few patterns in your fly boxes at all times, you'll cover an amazing number of summer situations that you would never even recognize as situations if you did not take time to get your nose down next to the water.

Beetles come in so many sizes and shapes and colors that you'd be busy for the rest of your life if you decided to imitate just a tenth of those that trout see and eat. Fortunately, like ants, they're easy to average. Most of them are black, or some shade so near it that trout are willing to take a black beetle imitation whenever they're feeding on beetles.

In fact, for some reason, trout will accept a black beetle pattern nearly any time they're feeding daintily on the surface, no matter what natural they happen to be taking. It's a critical concept to remember: whenever trout sip softly, you can nearly always bring them to a small beetle pattern even if you can't tell what they're taking. It might be a mayfly, a caddis, or a midge. It doesn't matter. Try to match it if you can. If you can't, try a #16 or smaller beetle pattern fished in the surface film. Most times it will work.

To notice when beetles bring about their own selective feeding, you'll need to repeat the ant experience and get your eyes as close to the water as you can. Better yet, suspend a small seine net half in and half out of the water. Hold it there for some time; nearly everything you do in the pursuit of late summer terrestrial fishing will have to be done with patience. Lift the seine and examine it closely. If you find beetles in the meshes, you can be quite certain trout are feeding on them, and you need to match them.

Matching beetles is not a difficult task. I'd recommend that you buy a small dry-fly box with eight to 10 tiny compartments and fill it with nothing but ant and beetle patterns. If you're like lots of other fly fishermen who spend much time fishing in the slow times of late summer over waters that have become reduced in size and are somewhat smooth on top, you'll come to call this your *bailout box*.

The box should contain the ant patterns I've already mentioned, in #14 to #20, black and cinnamon. Add beetles in black — toss in a few reddish-brown patterns if you'd like — and in the same sizes.

The Crowe Beetle is probably the most popular beetle pattern. It's tied with deer hair dyed black. A hank of the hair is wrapped bow to stern on the hook shank to form the body, then pulled forward over the body as the carapace, or shellback. The hair butts are clipped to leave a head over the eye of the hook. A few hair fibers are drawn out to each side and clipped short to represent the stubby legs of the natural beetle. The whole system comes from the same bundle of hair fibers. The fly floats the way you want a beetle to float: flush in the surface film. It's very difficult to see on the water, which means you've got to fish it on a short line, always an aid to delicate presentations.

Another design, the Featherwing Beetle, is based on Vince Marinaro's brilliant work, recorded in his *American Dry Fly Code* (Lyons & Burford, first published in 1950). The body is simply a dark hackle palmered over the hook shank and clipped top and bottom. The original wing was jungle cock tied flat over the hackle for the Jassid, Marinaro's most famous pattern. Any small, dark feather can be substituted for the jungle cock to make a black beetle.

You can construct a perfect Featherwing Beetle by stroking the fibers of a black hackle along the stem, reversing them, then catching the stem and fibers against the hook shank. Tie in the reversed feather just behind the hook eye. Treat it with Flexament. It's very simple, and very effective.

I consider Marinaro's book the most influential in American fly-fishing literature. You should read it. But when you do, focus on his ways of *observing* and his ways of *thinking* more than on the particular fly patterns he originated. The patterns are far from being out of date, but they're not as uni-

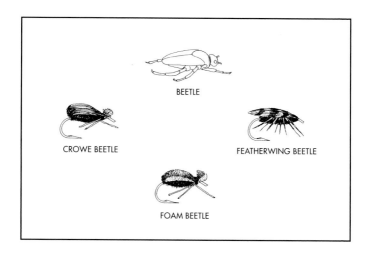

BEETLE

CROWE BEETLE

FEATHERWING BEETLE

FOAM BEETLE

Beetle and Imitations

versal as his observations and interpretations of what goes on in the world of trout.

Traditionalists will stick with the Crowe Beetle and Marinaro's Featherwings. Other anglers will prefer the Foam Beetle, tied with a fur body, palmered hackle trimmed on the bottom, and shellback of closed-cell foam. It looks alarmingly like a living beetle and floats amazingly well for a beetle pattern. It's an easy tie and it's easy to keep floating. Tied in #14 to #20, it's an excellent choice for your bailout box.

You'll encounter other terrestrials on the water, but not as often as hoppers, ants, and beetles. Inchworms, for example, dangle themselves toward disaster from streamside trees, on ropes of silk. Various box elder bugs and stink bugs and spiders also get into occasional trouble with trout. Few of these, however, do it on so regular a basis that you'll find it necessary to match them.

Concentrate on hoppers, ants, and beetles. They're the terrestrial insects that bring about the most consistent selective feeding. When you've got them covered, you've got most late-summer terrestrial situations solved.

The last thing to cover is tackle for presenting terrestrials. As you can imagine, it requires something different to propel a #10 dense hopper pattern in a high and hot wind than it does to delicately set a #18 ant onto the smooth surface of a breathless spring creek. This is a good moment to point out that you'll find fish feeding selectively on tiny ants and beetles only on waters where the surface is smooth. Where it's rough, these insects get tumbled under and taken deep.

Earlier in this book, I pointed out the need for a slightly stout outfit to fish searching dry flies: an 8 1/2 to 9-foot rod for a 5-weight line in calm country, a 6-weight where the wind blows. I also described the more delicate presentation outfit: a rod of the same length for a 3-weight line where the wind seldom blows, a 4 or 5-weight when wind becomes a factor. With those two outfits in mind, it's easy to figure out which one to use for these separate situations. For hoppers, use the heavier outfit. For finesse fishing with tiny ants and beetles, use the lighter gear. If you think you might encounter either in the same day, then carry a compromise outfit that will let you fish both.

It sometimes pays to set hoppers onto the water with a splat; trout are accustomed to the awkward arrivals of these clumsy fliers. The splat can even gain attention and prompt a quick boiling take. When fishing tinier ants and beetles, creep as close as you can to feeding fish, stay low, and cast as softly as possible. Any fly that is designed to float half in and half out of the water will not float at all if it lands with a whack.

That's all about late summer. Seek out shade. Shift your fishing to dawn and dusk. If you find fish sipping at midday or any other time but can't see anything on the surface, try ants and beetles from your bailout box. If trout are feeding boldly rather than sipping, toss a hopper and hold on.

The summer season divides into early and late periods even more clearly on lakes than it does on streams. This is not because flows become shallow and slow in the hot weather. Rather, it's because lakes stratify in summer, separating into a warm upper layer and a cool lower layer with an abrupt transition in between.

During the pre-stratification period of early summer, the water of a lake is mixed by the same currents that caused turnover in spring. Water temperatures remain relatively constant throughout all depths due to this mixing. The shallows are a few degrees warmer than the depths, because sun strikes the bottom in water just a few feet deep and confines all the solar energy to a restricted water column, heating it up. Currents continue to shift water from the depths to the shallows, however, so the heat in the shallows is slowly wicked off.

The difference in temperature remains minor in early summer, and shallows stay well within the comfort range of trout. As a result, trout remain in the relative shallows, say two to 10 feet deep, most of the time in the early summer season. That means June and most of July in the average temperate trout lake, into August in lakes farther north or at higher elevations, but ending in late June in lakes farther south or nearer sea level.

Before stratification sets in, trout behavior on stillwaters does not differ a great deal from what it was in the spring. Most trout foods are active in the shallows; trout go where they find food. And until something drives them out, that's where they stay.

In early summer, you'll continue to fish rises whenever and wherever you find them in stillwaters. You'll hit hatches of the same speckle-wing quill mayflies (*Callibaetis*) you fished in spring. In fact, they'll be the same species. Because of their

SPECKLE-WING MAYFLY   HARROP HAIRWING DUN

Speckle-Wing Mayfly and Imitation

constant environments, lakes do not harbor the varied hatches you find in streams.

Speckle-wings have a habit you need to know about. In spring, they come off as #12 duns, sometimes #14. You work out an imitation, as my friends and I did on Yellowstone Lake. We used #12 Olive Harrop Hairwing Duns. In early summer, the same species hatches around the same time of day: between 11:00 and 3:00. You go for it, and it's a great hatch, especially since you've already got it nailed, having fished this hatch in spring and matched it then.

You cast your fly out among the floating duns and the trout rising to take them, but nothing takes your fly. Why does the fly that worked for you in spring on the same species suddenly fail you in summer?

Speckle-wing mayflies go through two or three successive generations in the same year. The first emerges in spring; its nymphs have had all winter to feed and grow. They're large: usually #12, sometimes #14. That first generation mates and lays the eggs for the next generation, the one you'll fish in early summer. This class of nymphs, however, has only a few weeks to browse and reach full growth. If the first hatch comes off in April, the second hatch will arrive in mid to late June. That gives the nymphs just eight to 10 weeks to put on fat.

The result is a predictable one: nymphs of the second generation do not attain the same size as those of the first generation. If the first hatch of speckle-wing duns was a #12, which is most common, the second will be #14. If the earlier ones were #14, then the second generation will be #16. That's why you're not getting as much action, even though you're fishing the same fly over the same hatch. To solve the problem, simply drop your fly down one size, and you'll find yourself back in business with trout.

I'll give a fall hint here in the summer chapter: the same species will have a third hatch on many waters, in September or early October. It will once again be a full size smaller. So the same insect you match in spring with a #12 fly will be matched two generations later with a #16. If you don't notice this and don't reduce the size of your imitation, you'll very quickly see how the failure to change sizes affects your chances to catch trout.

Tactics for the speckle-wing hatch in summer are the same as those I outlined in the spring notes. Fish an Olive Hare's Ear Nymph in the morning, before the hatch. Switch over to a dry pattern such as the Olive Harrop Hairwing Dun only when you see that trout are feeding selectively on duns. If spinners fall, which they will, then you must make a third switch to a spentwing pattern.

I usually clip the wings and bottom hackles off an Adams to create a spinner pattern. But don't let yourself be fooled by the presence of hundreds, perhaps even thousands, of dancing speckle-wing spinners in the air. Those are males waiting for females to emerge from lakeside vegetation. The males don't get onto the water often, and it is quite uncommon for trout to take them.

Keep those binoculars handy. Watch to see what disappears in swirls. If it's duns, you know what to use. If it's distinctly spinners, then switch. If nothing goes down, suspect that trout are still feeding on speckle-wing nymphs or else taking a midge that you're having trouble spotting on the water.

So long as fishing is good, stick with what you are doing. As soon as you cease to get strikes on the fly you've been using, slow down and try to figure out what has changed. Observation is one of the most important pieces of lake fishing paraphernalia you can own, and you can't buy it at any price. Watch with binocs. Or lie on a log or the bank and look into the water. Poke your nose over the gunwale of your boat or the side of your float tube. Get close to the water, then focus on the surface and below it.

Even if this close observation doesn't pay off in the form of an instant solution to whatever problem you're trying to solve, such snooping will expand your knowledge about life in lakes. That knowledge will not fail to pay dividends over the ensuing days and weeks and seasons.

Other insects are important in early summer. Damselfly nymphs continue to migrate. You'll need to match them if you see them. At rare times, adult damselflies get blown to the water by high winds and are taken by trout. When this happens, you will catch more trout if you can match them. Midges also keep coming off. Like speckle-wing mayflies, they have several generations per year, and their size drops as spring turns to summer turns to fall. You'll want to use the same flies I discussed in the spring chapter, but you'll need to drop them down a size a season as time marches on.

Caddis begin hatching in lakes and ponds in the early summer season. This is their time of importance. You might never know about them, though, if you aren't on the lake at dawn and dusk.

Many stillwater caddis emerge and simply sit for a little while to let their new wings dry before they fly away. These species can be imitated with the same set of elk-hair and quill-wing flies I recommended for stream caddis. It's wise to con-

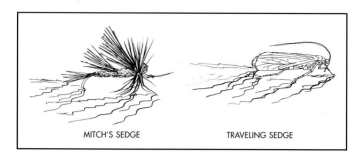

Traveling Sedge and Imitation

sider clipping the hackles from the bottom of your caddis imitations, however, when you use them in a stillwater situation. You have no need for extra flotation, and you're better off without the hackle because it distorts the silhouette of the imitation. An Elk-Hair Caddis, for example, is excellent on streams because it rides the water on the tiptoes of its hackle. But if you clip the hackles off at the bottom, the same fly floats flush in the surface and becomes an excellent lake pattern during caddis hatches.

Some lake caddis display a unique behavior that you must match more closely than the insect's appearance if you hope to fool any fish while these particular species are out. They're called *traveling sedges*. They emerge in the surface film like any other caddis. Once they get there, though, they start motoring around rather than taking off. This is crazy behavior, and trout know about it.

If you choose a fly such as the Mitch's Sedge, which is designed to be able to skate, you won't have to worry about how much it looks like the real caddis sitting on the water. Trout key on this movement, not the sedge's shape. Whenever you see caddis boating the water and trout taking them off the surface with a smack, tie on a skating dry. An Elk-Hair Caddis will do if you have nothing nearer, but it's best if it's hackled, not trimmed. Let it sit after the cast, then draw it across the surface in a series of retrieves three to five feet long.

Trout will normally take the fly on the move, not the sit. If you see signs of a fish after the fly, such as a bulge or "V"-shaped wake welling up behind it, don't stop the retrieve or the trout might turn away. Traveling sedges are large, usually #8 to #12. They come off most often just after daylight or just before dark.

In early summer, many stillwater hatches shift out of the center of the day to either early morning or late afternoon and evening. It's not a bad program to take a leisurely lunch, even a snooze if you'd like, but don't do this if speckle-wings are hatching. The center of the day is when they're most active.

Whenever you're on a lake in early summer, before stratification sets in, and you see no surface activity, suspect that trout are still in the shallows, but down near the bottom. This is precisely the behavior I mentioned in the chapter on spring. Nothing has changed; look for that lake intersection. Choose a generic green fly, count it down six to 10 feet deep on a wet-tip or wet-head line, and retrieve it slowly. You'll catch fish.

STRATEGIES FOR STRATIFIED STILLWATERS

Only lakes of some size and depth stratify. Ponds rarely stratify because few are deep enough to form layers in the water column. Lakes less than about 12 feet deep also fail to stratify because the wind is generally strong enough to mix such shallow water.

Your average trout lake, which has enough acreage to be interesting and enough depth to provide cool sanctuary to trout, does stratify. If you fish lakes a lot, it's a situation you will see every summer and will need to handle whenever you go fishing after the weather has turned consistently hot.

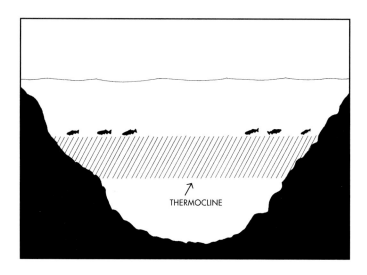

Stratified Lake

Stratification is caused by the varying density of water at different temperatures. Cooler and denser water settles toward the bottom, and warmer and less dense water rises toward the surface. Sometime in mid to late summer the difference in density becomes so great that it forms an abrupt barrier between light water on top and dense water below.

This abrupt barrier, called the *thermocline,* forms in most trout lakes between 15 and 25 feet down. The larger and deeper the lake, the deeper the thermocline. The smaller and shallower the lake, the shallower the thermocline.

Water above the thermocline has plenty of oxygen due to wind mixing, but it becomes too warm for trout. Water below the thermocline is cool, but it lacks enough oxygen for trout. When the water warms to 70 degrees F. and beyond, trout begin their movement out and down toward the thermocline from the area along the shoreline. They stop when they reach the level of cooler water just above the thermocline.

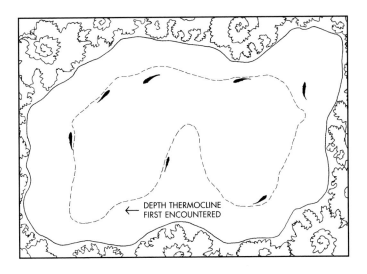

Distribution of Trout in Stratified Lake

They end up suspended in somewhat of a ragged circle around the lake at the depth where they first encountered the thermocline as they moved away from shore. You'd be crazy to think trout are lined up in a circle around a lake as neatly as tarpon in a daisy chain. But you'd also be crazy to disregard the fact that there's a pattern to where trout hold in a lake stratified in the heat of late summer.

You find suspended trout in one of three ways. The first, which I'm just beginning to experiment with, is by using depth finders, many of which can also spot fish. I always feel a little like I'm cheating when I look for structure and trout with a depth finder. I might decide it's unfair, for me. You must define these things for yourself. So long as you promise to release your trout, I don't mind your pursuit of these experiments as well. Let me know what you discover.

The second way to find suspended fish is to search for the thermocline by lowering and raising a thermometer often enough to locate the level where the water suddenly shifts a few degrees in temperature. That tells you the depth to fish: just above the shift.

The third way, the way I've always done it and feel best about doing it, is the patient search of the water column with a trolled fly. I enjoy float tubing, and I love my eight-foot pram. I can be content with long bouts of towing a fly, or, as I mentioned in the spring chapter, a pair of them.

Fly pattern is not nearly as important in trolling as depth fished. I've always had good luck with black or olive Woolly Buggers, in #8 or #10. If you have a favorite fly for lakes, use it. Don't spend time trolling or casting a fly you don't know trout will take when you finally get it in front of them.

As in spring, you're searching for an intersection. This time it's farther out from shore and deeper down. You're not likely to find it with a wet-tip line. Instead, choose a 30-foot wet-head in extra-fast sinking, or a full-sinking line. I prefer a shooting-head system that has lines in three sink rates: fast, extra-fast, and ultra-fast. Most of my fishing over stratified lakes is done with the extra-fast head, but I don't wait long before looping on the ultra-fast if I have trouble finding fish.

You can cast and use the countdown method, rather than trolling, to search for suspended trout when a lake is stratified. Begin your counts at 20 seconds; extend them to a minute or more. The standard count should be about 60 seconds. If it gets longer than that, go to a line with a faster sink rate. Finding fish by casting and counting your fly down at this time of year is going to take lots of time unless you're luckier than I am. That's why I prefer to troll.

Trolling has a practical advantage over casting when you're searching for suspended trout. The fly is kept at depth constantly, rather than being passed through the depths and then lifted out of them for the next cast and count. That becomes a huge advantage when trout are tough to find.

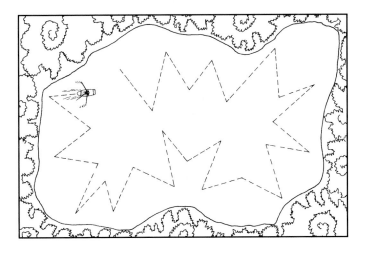

Trolling Pattern on Stratified Lake

Never simply circle the lake a set distance from shore. To make sure you cross the rough circular line where suspended trout hold, set up a zigzag trolling pattern. Troll in toward shore, then head out away from it.

It's also necessary to change the depth at which you search. You can do this by switching lines to change the sink rate. You can do it a lot more conveniently by changing your trolling speed every quarter hour or so. Kick up the speed to lift the fly; slow down to let it drop. At times, stop completely to get the fly as deep your line allows. Then ease off slowly to keep it down there long enough to explore a zig or a zag across that imaginary line where trout might hold.

That's all: vary your distance from shore constantly. Vary the sink rate of your line. Vary the speed at which you explore for fish. And once you've found trout, stick with them. Note reference points on shore and triangulate your location as soon as you can after you've had a hit. Play out the fish, then return to where you hooked it.

Whenever you hook a trout, troll back through the area time after time, from one direction, then another. Try to remember how much line you had out and how fast you were flippering or rowing. Your goal is to troll the same fly through the same spot at the same depth and speed. If you manage that, it's probable that other trout are in the same place for the same reasons. They'll see the fly and inhale it.

Once you've found the solution to finding the first fish on a stratified lake, you should be able to find more. You'll continue to need patience, however, to corral them.

SUMMER PREPARATION

I don't know how many summer days I've had ruined by weather, which can be perfectly pleasant and still cause problems. I hope you can learn from my mistakes.

The largest of these mistakes is wearing a baseball cap rather than a hat that protects my nose and ears from sun, especially the rays that are reflected off the water. A wide-brimmed cowboy hat works well, but the up-downer is a great one, too. Don't forget that you can tuck a bandanna up under a baseball cap in back and drape it over your ears and the nape of your neck. If you get hot, dip the bandanna in water, wring it out, and tuck it in again.

Wear long-sleeved shirts to keep off the sun and mosquitoes. I usually wear cotton shirts of the kind some makers call *canvas*. The material is cool, but thick enough to repel probing proboscises. If the weather is hot and mosquitoes are not a problem, wear a synthetic, quick-drying tropical shirt. But these shirts are not good against rain or wind.

The best protection from sudden summer showers, and also from summer winds that spring up and chill you, is a light windbreaker with a hood. It should be water-repellent.

If you're fishing country where thunderstorms are a daily menace, exchange the windbreaker for a waterproof slicker. If lightning begins to strike near enough to make you nervous, get away from anything tall, such as a tree, and lower your own profile. If you're in a boat or tube, get off the water.

I leave my neoprene waders home in summer unless I'm wading water so dangerous I want them for flotation. Most often, I wear lightweight waders in summer and vary what's under them according to the temperature of the water. If it's cool, I'll wear polypro long handles. If it's warm, I'll wear cotton. If the water temperature allows it, I'll often wade wet.

Be sure to carry mosquito repellent and sunblock in your vest. Add lip balm that contains sunscreen. I once went on a five-day fishing trip around Yellowstone Lake, rowing a boat day after day. Fishing was terrific, and I'd do it again in an instant. But my lips became blistered, and they stayed painful for days. My lip balm lacked sunscreen, and my lips got badly sunburned. Don't make that mistake.

One especially important item that I always have ready in summer is an all-around fly box that I keep in my pickup at all times, in a belt bag that also holds a reel. I hide it behind the seat with a pack rod and a pair of hip boots.

The all-around fly box contains a few of my favorite and most dependable dries, nymphs, streamers, and wets: just a few dozen flies. That's not a lot, but they're the ones I know will take fish in nearly any situation. With this minimum of gear always handy, I can stop whenever I find myself near water, and go off to explore it.

Even if you catch few trout and they're not large ones, exploration can bring about some of the most adventurous summer fishing of all. If your summer doesn't include at least a small measure of adventure, it's been largely wasted.

OVERLEAF: *Preparing to fish Flat Creek, Jackson Hole.*

CHAPTER FOUR

FALL

I just returned from an October trip that confirmed a theory I've developed about small-stream trout fishing. I've noticed that in spring and early summer trout depend on aquatic insects for food. These hatch in riffles and runs and are delivered to trout at the heads of pools. In late summer and fall, aquatic hatches taper off and trout turn to terrestrials. These drop from streamside to the broad bodies of pools and collect at the funnels that are the tailouts.

According to my theory, small-stream trout hold at the heads of pools early in the year, lower toward the tailouts of pools later in the year.

This idea came to me after I had gone through many years of fall frustration on my small home stream. In the spring and summer, I could nearly always wade out to the middle of a pool, make a cast to the current tongue feeding into the head of it, and raise willing trout to my dry flies. As the fishing season progressed, however, I became astonished at the number of times I frightened fish before I got into position to make my first cast. They would arrow off the thin tailout the instant I showed myself at the lower end of a pool. I would cast but catch nothing.

I began stalking those small pools much more carefully as the season wore on. I got into the habit of kneeling at the foot of a pool and making my first casts to the narrowing and gathering currents there. I was surprised at the sudden increase in my luck. I took lots of trout out of water so thin it looked like it would not even cover their dorsal fins.

One day I spent as much time stalking pools and peering into them with binoculars as I did casting to them with flies. It's an assignment you should give yourself. That day was a trout-fishing education. The sun struck through the water and illuminated the bottom. Trout crouched visibly among the stones, in the thin water where the currents began to gather. They lifted up and shot forward to examine every leaf and twig and insect that fell to the surface of the pool. As I watched, it occurred to me that trout so deployed would be able to intercept anything that arrived on the pool. Had they held at the head of the pool where they were fed best in spring, everything would have landed behind them and they'd have never known it.

It also occurred to me that those trout were exposed to predation in that shallow, clear water. They seemed aware of this and very nervous about it.

When trout hold in the inches-deep water at the foot of a pool, they're so easily frightened that you're forced to stalk them in a crouch or on hands and knees. You must also cast to them with your rod canted to the side and in a way that keeps the line from flying over their heads. If you accomplish that, then they're not at all fussy about fly pattern. They're primed to take whatever lands on the water and looks buggy.

If you fail to accomplish any of this, and send the trout flying, then they will startle all the other fish in their rush up the pool. The result will be the same I used to achieve when I stepped to the middle of a pool to make my first cast: no trout caught.

How was I able to confirm my theory? By spending a week backpacking along a small stream that arises high on a snow-capped mountain out in the Oregon desert. The first day, every time I approached a pool with the carelessness one assigns trout in such a remote location, two or three "V"-shaped wakes shot off the tailouts. These were obviously frightened trout, which I proved by then casting to the pools and accomplishing the familiar result: catching nothing.

Over the next few days, I initiated a series of small experiments. The first was to see what percentage of pools had trout at the tailouts and what percentage had trout at their heads. Every pool with a long, flat center part — the body of the pool — had several trout holding in its lower half. I discovered something else during this experiment. When I cast to the plunge pools and pocket water immediately upstream and down from the long flat pools, I found them literally empty. It's too early to confirm my new theory that trout migrate from these spring and summer lies to the longer pools because the broader expanse of water catches larger numbers of terrestrial insects. It's enough to know that I caught trout in the flats and tailouts of long pools and rarely anywhere else.

My next experiment was to walk casually and in full view up to each pool. I wanted to see when those arrows would fire off the tailouts. I was able to confirm some earlier research that I wrote about in *Tactics for Trout* (Stackpole Books, 1990) and will condense here. Light striking water at an angle below 10 degrees is reflected, and trout cannot see anything beneath that 10-degree line of vision. (See next page for illustration.) If you're 40 feet from a trout, you can stand up and still be invisible because the light delivering your image to the water is below the 10-degree angle and is therefore reflected. If you're 30 feet from a trout, you must crouch to stay out of sight. If you're 20 feet from it, you must kneel. At 10 feet, you need to be on hands and knees. If you're any closer than that, you've got to be on your belly.

I had always considered these figures more important for fishing smooth water over selective trout. Now I know they have considerable importance for the angler on any water.

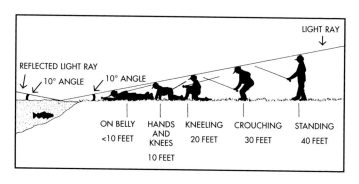

Trout's 10-Degree Line of Vision

My final experiment involved getting the fly onto the water without wasting the effort of a careful approach. Needless to say, casting with my rod directly overhead negated all my efforts to keep my body down low to the ground. That vertical rod sent them sailing. I had to tip it over and cast sidearm. You also know the results of draping the line over the heads of trout holding in six inches of water. That also shot them off. I was finally able to fool them only when I cast with the leader and fly landing on the water and the line draped over rocks or the bank at the tailout of the pool. This had the added advantage of canceling drag, which is a constant problem on any tailout.

These three experiments told me where the trout held, how best to approach them, and how to make a cast that would not frighten them. With those major problems solved, I discovered that fly selection was a very minor factor. If the fly landed on the water and sat there looking somewhat alive, trout would shoot forward and sip it in. I was surprised by the gentleness of the takes, and yet also surprised by the determination of them. The fish were on and solidly hooked. A splashy rise, as I've pointed out earlier, is often not a sign of eagerness but a change of mind.

You can see how vastly different small-stream tactics are for fall fishing as compared to tactics for the same streams in spring and early summer. You approach the foot of the pool rather than its head. You creep carefully rather than arriving erect. And you must cast cautiously rather than laying your line right up the center of the turbulent current tongue that earlier in the year served to conceal you and your line and any mistakes you might have made. Some of the above small-stream research applies to larger streams, rivers, or even stillwater, too. I've got a favorite medium-sized stream that has in the past presented a nearly unsolvable problem. It's a forested stream, and in most places it has a steep gradient, bounding from plunge to plunge, hesitating occasionally and only long enough for trout to find resting places. I catch them in those fast lies with dry flies.

The same stream has a half-mile-long level stretch that is still densely forested but has a series of long, flat pools broken by the gentlest of riffles. Because the riffles are nearly as flat as the pools, they offer no cover behind which you can approach close to a tailout and cast short without frightening the fish. Nor do the wide tailouts offer rocks you can drape the line tip over while laying the leader and fly onto the water.

On a medium-sized to large stream, when trout hang on tailouts in shallow water, it's tough to get near enough to present a fly to them. In addition, they're protected by the same funnel effect that delivers their food. Your fly lands upstream from your line, higher in the funnel where the current is slower. The line, landing on faster water, is instantly whisked away, dragging the fly behind it. A wiggle cast might solve it, but you can't introduce much wiggle into a 15-foot cast.

I found a solution to these low-water situations that can be applied on trout in streams of any size, a solution I've also been able to apply in late summer. It works whenever trout are holding low in pools and are bashful about being there.

The first part of the solution is to approach from upstream. This puts you in an awkward position because trout hold facing upstream. They're watching for their food to land on the pool up there. If you enter their field of vision or send your line sailing over their heads, you will be taken aback when the trout seem to charge you. They'll arrow off that tailout right toward their nearest sanctuary, the current tongue that is now right at your feet. Once they get there, you're not going to catch them. You must deliver your fly without the trout knowing you're there.

The first part of solving that problem is keeping below the 10-degree line of vision. The second part is approaching without sending any wading waves ahead of you. Usually that means you should stay on shore if it's at all possible. If it's not, you're going to have to move at a creep, because we're talking about shallow pools here, and nothing magnifies wading waves like still and thin water.

Once you're in position to make your cast, then the best thing to do might come as a mild surprise to you. Those trout are on the tailout in fall watching for the arrival of any insect that might land on the pool upstream. But they're also interested in gathering all the nutrients they can for the coming winter. Lots of those nutrients take the form of sculpins. Most folks think these small fish live mostly in pools. I've made the mistake of thinking that, and even writing about it, myself. It's not true. Sculpins prefer fast, clean currents where detritus gets funneled to them. They love tailouts, just like trout. They dart from stone to stone, hugging the bottom, hiding among pebbles and stones.

That should give you a hint about what to do when approaching trout on a tailout in a medium-sized to large stream. Nip off your dry fly and tie on a small streamer in its place. A #10 or #12 Muddler works perfectly for this kind of fishing. It should be very lightly weighted, if at all. If your pattern sim-

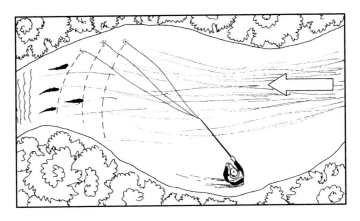

Fishing a Thin Tailout in Fall

ply sinks and sits on the bottom of the stream, it can't do what you want it to do.

What you want it to do is the same thing those sculpins spend their time doing: dart from rock to rock across the tailout. Here's how to make it happen: from your crouch up near the head of the pool and off to one side, cast across so the fly lands almost on the far bank. In fall that's a potential lie, and your fly might get pounced. If it doesn't, swing the fly across the pool five or six feet above the tailout. Let the current draw it across. Don't let it swim fast, and never with a steady motion. Use a staccato movement of your rod tip to make the fly start and stop. Swim it across the top of the tailout stumbling and stuttering.

This approach and presentation does more than imitate the movement of the natural sculpin. It puts the pattern in front of the trout, with no line and leader between the fly and the fish as would have been the case if you had cast upstream with a dry fly. By approaching from upstream and casting down, you are able to cover all of the lies along the tailout without frightening any of the fish.

You'll be surprised how far the fish will move to take the fly. That's why you start by casting a few feet above the tailout. Often you'll simply feel a jerk. Most times, though, you'll see one of those arrows start off the tailout and shoot right at your fly. If you can keep from jerking the fly out of there once in a while, you have more discipline than I do.

If no trout come to the first cast, make your second cast a foot or so farther down the current, and fish the fly stuttering and stumbling along. As it approaches closer to the lip of the pool on subsequent casts, it travels in shallower and shallower water. That's why you don't want the fly to be heavily weighted.

On a large river, trout hold in the same kind of water for the same reasons. But the tailout is likely to be deeper. In that case, a wet-tip line and short leader help you get the fly to the bottom, which is where it needs to be, because that's where those sculpins do all of their traveling. Increase the size of the fly if you'd like, though the small one will do just as well. But don't use a heavily weighted fly, because the excess lead will kill the action. You still want the fly to stumble and dart along. With that goal in mind, wade into a position that lets you angle the fly deep and slow and erratically along the bottom of the tailout. Be patient. It takes a lot more casts to cover all of the potential holding water on a large tailout.

The size trout you're quite likely to catch when you employ this technique on a large river makes being out in fall a very worthwhile way to spend your time.

FALL AS A TRANSITION TIME

Early fall usually continues the rhythms of late summer. The weather remains hot. Aquatic insect hatches remain subdued and continue to occur around dawn and dusk. The shape of your fishing day in early September should be the same as it was in August, the dead center of summer. Get out on the stream early, when the water is cool after the short night. Watch for insect activity and for trout rising to feed on whatever is hatching or is returning to the water to lay eggs.

Continue to fish until it gets hot and activity begins to dwindle. Then take your own rest. Eat a long lunch, nap in the shade of a tree, if you'd like, or just be watchful. As I mentioned in the last chapter, all it takes is a little insect activity to stir up a little trout activity, even when all other conditions seem stacked against anything positive happening.

As the sun tips over into the evening part of its arc, take up your rod and your staff again and begin prowling the water. That's the time of day when trout, feeling the coolness gathering, also begin to prowl.

Your early fall day has the same shape as your late summer day: fish early and late, take it easy in between. But recall that streams with steady temperatures below the stress levels of trout have no slack in activity at any time of the day, so long as trout have something around to stir their interest. That usually means terrestrials in the fall of the year. On spring creeks and meadow streams, you'll often notice the presence of a particular hopper, beetle, or ant species, in which case you must match it to catch many trout.

On forested streams, fall is a time of restlessness for many types of insects — certain beetles, some spiders, lots of termites, a few flying ants, inchworms dangling from silken threads; the list can go on and on. You get the idea already, though: trout are suddenly seeing a wide variety of things falling from the forested banks. Mixed in with the terrestrials are a lot of aquatic insect species returning to lay their eggs during this last chance of the year. A preponderance of these returning insects are caddis, for the simple reason that adult

OVERLEAF: *Jim Schollmeyer on the Siletz River in Oregon.*

Brush Hatches

caddis live a few weeks and do their egg-laying chores over a wide span of time. Ephemeral mayflies come off in intense hatches and mate in dramatic spinner flights, in part because they're so short-lived and must therefore synchronize their activities so that they're all together in the same brief time. When that time is over, you don't see many mayflies. But caddis continue to deposit eggs in good numbers almost daily.

Through the middle part of the day, it's wise to watch for terrestrial falls. If a particular species dominates, then attempt to match it. If a scattering of species is around, then use searching flies to take trout. Toward evening, look for return flights of egg-laying caddis.

I'd like to bring up a concept that I consider to be of minor importance throughout the earlier seasons, but of prime importance in the fall of the year. It's what I call *brush hatches,* and it refers to the general run and rush of things that pour out of streamside vegetation and hover over the water, sometimes at midday, more often at evening.

Brush hatches can be evening spinner falls of mayflies. You'll see a few insects dancing in the air, nothing on the water, but you'll see trout rising and sipping something gently. Those are the female spinners, lying spent and nearly invisible in the surface film. It's time to get out your collecting net and start seining the currents. You'll have to find a match to do much good.

A brush hatch can also be a fall dispersal flight of flying termites or an awkward abundance of long-legged craneflies making sorties over the water. Trout become aware of these minor presences, which are just enough to keep the fish tuned in and looking toward the surface. You can nearly always take advantage of this kind of activity with searching dry flies.

The most common kind of brush hatch is an egg-laying flight of caddisflies. And now we're suddenly back to a problem addressed earlier: caddis in the air, splashy rises on the water, but a general lack of interest in your dry flies. I don't need to say any more; these caddis are diving down to lay their eggs, and you'll begin catching fish as soon as you switch from the matching dry fly to a wet fly that is an estimate of what you see in the air. That's all it takes. But these brush hatches can give you fits until you realize that it's often best to match the aerial insect with a wet fly that looks a little like it.

When the heat of summer finally lets up, streams and their environments begin shifting their daily rhythms. The shift, as you might suspect, is the reverse of what happened as the seasons progressed from early spring to late spring, then through early and late summer. Those shifts moved activity from the warmest part of the day to the coolest: dawn and dusk. The shift that occurs between early and late fall condenses the reversal into a few weeks. Sometimes it happens in a few days, prompted by the first burst of bad weather.

As the weather cools, either slowly or abruptly, most activity during the day shifts from dawn and dusk back to midmorning and mid-afternoon, and then finally to where it was in the earliest part of the season: right in the middle of the day when the water is at its warmest. You must also shift your own rhythms with the change in activity, or you'll find yourself trying to play the game when the trout have no interest in playing it with you.

It's not difficult to tell when you should begin shifting. When dawn and dusk become uncomfortably cool for you, they're also uncomfortable for insects and trout. Watch to see when insects are active. Brush hatches are especially easy to notice. When craneflies and caddis and even mayfly spinners begin shifting their returns to the water from dusk to mid-afternoon, you know it's time to give up your long lunches and brief naps. Watch for rising trout. Their activity will obviously follow that of the insects. You'll start to see them at midday rather than in early morning and late evening. Concentrate your fishing, as you did in spring, on the time of day when the weather is warmest.

FALL CHANCES WHEN THE WEATHER REVERTS TO CHILL

When the shift from summer rhythms to the fall cycle is complete, the stream's day and your own day will return to about what they were in post-runoff spring. But you won't benefit from the intense hatches that enlivened the middle of the day at that time of year.

You'll do well fishing nymphs in middle to late morning, watching for emergences or brush hatches in the center part of the day, then switching to nymphs, wet flies, or streamers as the heat wanes in late afternoon. The rhythm is the same as spring, but hatches tend to be scant. Trout are hungry, though, which is why fishing nymphs or streamers pays off in trout caught during this season of the year.

Even after insects dwindle, fall continues to be a good time to explore tailouts with Muddlers and other streamers. At this time of year, trout see fewer small items to bite and are interested in storing energy for the long winter ahead. That makes them most vulnerable to big bites such as streamers.

You might be surprised how far a trout will move to take a streamer in the fall. That's one reason you'll do fairly well even if you fish a floating line and let the streamer ride high in the currents. You might also be surprised how many trout you fail to catch by doing this. You'll catch some trout when you fish the streamer wrong — high in the water and fast — but you'll catch many more when you fish it right. That requires using the right line, wet-tip or otherwise, to get the fly near the bottom at the depth of water you're fishing.

Once you've got the streamer there, fish it slowly. When you fish a tailout, your goal is to stumble and stutter the streamer in the thin water. When you fish a streamer in any depth of water in fall, stumble and stutter it down near the bottom. Intersperse the movements with moments when the fly merely drifts along, somewhat like a crippled sculpin. That's what trout hope to see and will believe they see in your fly if you fish it right.

Brown trout make their spawning runs in fall, and everybody knows that big browns eat other fish, including other browns. They're hungry for streamers in late September, all of October, and into early November.

Most folks think of brown trout migrations as taking place only out of large lakes, up into the streams that feed them. The obvious and most famous example is the brown trout spawning run from Hebgen Lake into the upper Madison River. A few similar situations occur on the Missouri River, the upper Deschutes, and in a limited number of smaller fisheries that are less well known. These runs take place wherever lakes interrupt the courses of rivers. That nearly always means a dam, with a large reservoir, and the river entering at the upper end. Look for the spawning run above it. You're likely to find a crowd of fish and folks.

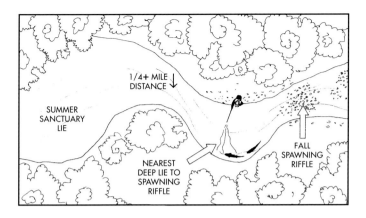

Finding Big Browns in Fall

Too few people realize that the same restlessness drives brown trout out of their deep holding lies on any stream or river and sends them into shallower water, where you might very well have your only opportunity of the season to get a fly in front of them.

I could name a dozen streams where this happens, but I'm not going to because I want to fish them myself and I don't want to find a crowd when I get there. You can easily find your own. Wherever you fish moving water that has resident brown trout, you'll find them spread out in shallower water and more vulnerable to your flies in the fall of the year. If you'd like to reduce finding them to somewhat of a science, then think about those sanctuary pools you've tried to fish all spring and summer but couldn't pry any trout out of, on account of water depth or protective cover or an undercut bank. If something weren't protecting them, they wouldn't be there and they wouldn't be so big.

Return to these pools in fall and look for the nearest potential spawning gravel. Explore it with streamers. Better still, look around for the closest minor cover to the riffle or run you think might attract the trout. That's where they'll be cowering during the day.

Send a streamer nosing through the area. You'll anger those cranky trout. They'll attack it.

As you can imagine, you won't guess right every single time on every bit of water you fish with this technique. When you do get it right, however, you're likely to be in for the biggest battle of your year.

There's no thrill quite like the thrill you get from hooking a big brown trout when it's far from the bomb shelter it's been using to thwart every angler for all the years it's taken the fish to grow so large.

When the weather has reverted to what we expect in fall, cold nights and weakly warm days, then you should think about whatever method it takes to get your flies to the bottom. That means split-shot and indicator nymphing, or the stuttered streamer fished on a sinking line.

Never discount the possibility of a fall hatch. It should arrive as no surprise that, as the weather cools and the daily rhythms revert to those of early spring, the hatches themselves follow the same cycle. I mentioned early in the book that little olive mayflies, in the genus *Baetis*, have their greatest importance in late winter and early spring, and again in fall. The same is true for midges in moving water.

Little olive hatches occur in the middle of chilly autumn days. If the day is bright and sunny, the hatch is most likely to be intense but brief. You might get only an hour or two of opportunity over rising and feeding fish. If the day is overcast, and it is even raining softly, the hatch will be less intense but might go on for hours. This is the best of all possibilities, because the trout keep feeding and are not as particular about the stage of the insect they'll accept. I won't repeat everything I wrote about fishing the hatch here. Use the flies and repeat the tactics that worked for you in spring.

Midge hatches go on all summer. Trout feed on them and you'll find a few times when you need to match them. But most of the time, on moving water, they're small enough and sporadic enough that this is rarely necessary. In autumn that changes. Why? Because the short warm period of the day condenses the emergence. The midges hatch over a two or three-hour period rather than all day. The numbers that result are enough to make them interesting to trout, which have also been deprived of most of their mayfly, stonefly, caddisfly, and terrestrial distractions.

Trout feed on midges in fall the same way they did in spring: sipping them quietly in the eddies and edge currents where the energy needed to take the tiny insects is minimal. You won't find trout fighting a heavy current to feed on midges. So concentrate your search for rises in what I described at the beginning of the book as the soft spots in the stream. Trout will concentrate their feeding in such easy water; you'll have to observe the water closely because the rises will be subtle.

Once you've spotted the fish, use the same flies and tactics I outlined earlier to fool some smutting trout.

LAKE STRATEGIES AS THE SEASON WINDS DOWN

In fall, a true turnover completely reverses the layers of a stratified lake. The upper layer, in contact with the chilled night air, cools and increases in density. When equilibrium in density is reached between the layer above the thermocline and the layer below it, the upper layer almost abruptly penetrates the lower layer and forces it upward.

This reversal has the same effect as the stirring caused by spring storms: it delivers nutrients into the shallows and oxygen into the depths. Trout are suddenly able to be anywhere in the lake they'd like.

Where they like to be is where the most food hangs out.

If you've already guessed that this area is the shallows down to the limits of light, you're running out of the need for lessons from me.

You won't come across many hatches at this time of year on lakes and ponds. Aquatic insects have generally laid their eggs in order to give the next generation a jump on life before winter arrives. Terrestrial insects have made their dispersal flights and finished their business. You'll probably encounter the last scattered hatches of the speckle-wing mayflies. Don't forget that each successive generation is smaller than the one before it, so you'll likely need to use the same fly that worked in spring — whether nymph, dun, or spinner — but in #16 rather than #12.

You'll also encounter the last trickle of midges. If trout feed on them, then match them. Their diminution in size is not as dramatic as that of the mayflies, so the patterns you've used to fish them in spring and summer might work perfectly in fall, without any decrease in size. But it's best to collect a pupa if you can, or scoop up a cast pupal skin, and compare its size to the fly you select.

If hatches are scattered, and trout rise to them sporadically, you'll be very smart to offer the fish two flies. When fishing over the mayfly hatch, tie a nymph as a dropper behind the dry that matches the dun. If it's a midge hatch, tie a midge-pupa pattern behind an adult imitation, or use the mayfly-dun pattern to suspend the midge nymph.

Trout are generally hungry in the fall and are less likely to be selective. At times you can succeed with any generic dry fly, nymph, or wet. But it's always best to match a hatch if one is occurring.

In fall, most trout will not be feeding on hatches but rather on the kinds of food forms that are in the water throughout the year. These include some of the most interesting creatures, and I'd like to describe them briefly, along with fly patterns that match them.

Scuds might be most important. They are abundant in nearly all stillwaters and so prolific in some lakes that trout feed on them almost exclusively all year round. They live in weedbeds and along the bottom in the shallows, wherever they have some sort of vegetation to browse on and some oxygen to fuel their fitful subaquatic flights. They are crustaceans and come in sizes too small to imitate, up to some that are half an inch long. You'll usually do best imitating them with #12 and #14 olive or gray scud patterns.

Scuds are curved when you capture them and hold them in your hand. When swimming in the water, they're straight as sticks, and your fly patterns should reflect that. Since they're nearly always found around vegetation, look first for weedbeds, then rig to deliver your chosen fly to the same level at which you find them. That nearly always means using a wet-tip, wet-belly, or wet-head line. I use the extra-fast line in my shooting-head system if my wet-tip won't reach the level of a weedbed.

Use the countdown method to deliver your scud pattern down to the weedbeds. The count will vary from 10 to 30 seconds. Once you're ticking weeds, shorten the count a few seconds and begin your search for hungry trout.

Scuds are rather rudderless swimmers and motor about in bursts. A retrieve made in very short strips imitates this action, though you should be sure to intersperse some hand-twist retrieves and pauses. Whatever you do, don't retrieve so fast that you lift the fly up and away from the level of the weedbed tops.

Leeches are always around, and trout are always greedy to get one. That's because leeches are the largest and juiciest morsels a trout is likely to encounter during a day's travels. The few stomach samples I've taken from large stillwater trout

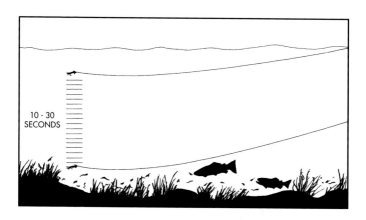

Counting a Scud or Leech Pattern Down to Weedbeds

nearly always reveal one or two leeches. Rarely do trout get the opportunity to feed selectively on them. Just as rarely do they pass up the chance to whack one.

If you set out to collect leeches, you'll find they come in sizes from half an inch long to a full three or four inches. My experience and the experience of others indicate it's leeches around two inches long that end up in a trout's stomach. I can't tell you why. You'd think the fish would prefer the largest they could get, but that is not the case. So stick with #6 to #10 leech patterns for most of your stillwater fishing in fall.

Most leeches I've seen are dark olive, black, tan, or blood red. My favorite patterns for them are olive or black Woolly Buggers. And I wouldn't want to spend a lot of time on lakes without a Blood Leech pattern handy. The best is tied with Canadian Mohair teased out to trail behind the hook shank.

Leeches spend most of their time idling along the bottom. That's the area where you should present your flies, but not necessarily at that speed. It's reasonable to assume that when a blind leech senses the approach of a predatory trout, it turns on its afterburners. Leeches might amble along most of the time, but when they're chased by trout, it's likely they're swimming in their undulatory fashion as fast as they can. So you should fish their imitations in one of two ways: hand twisted slowly, or trotted with a fast strip. Either way, you must remember one bit of trout behavior when fishing with a leech pattern. Biologist Paul Bech, a fishing partner on various Canadian expeditions, explained this to me. I immediately put it to the test and found Paul right.

It goes like this: a trout takes a leech by rushing in, opening its mouth, and flaring its gills to create suction. The leech is drawn right into the trout's open maw. So what happens when a trout rushes up behind your leech pattern, opens its mouth, and flares its gills? Nothing, because the pattern is tethered to your leader, and you're towing it along. "All you feel is a pluck," Paul told me. "So now all you should do is let go of the line."

It makes sense. The disappointed trout flares its gills again, and your released fly inserts itself where you want it. The trout turns away, you feel a strong pull, and only then do you set the hook. It works. I'd like to have the discipline to make it work every time. I don't. But when you can refrain from jerking on the rod after that initial pluck and drop the rod tip instead, most times, as Paul says, "you'll have your fish!"

One more thing and I'll quit rambling on about this final season on stillwaters. Trout are hungry at this time of year, and they're not finding a lot to satisfy that hunger. Consequently, they cruise restlessly. You see one rise a hundred feet away from you. You take off after it. Then a second trout rises a hundred feet in the opposite direction. You reverse field and paddle or flipper madly after it. Just as you get into range of where it was, the first fish rises again, so you charge back to where you started. Don't do that. Put on your brakes and simply sit awhile. Let things sort themselves out and you're likely to hook both of those bounders.

Trout in the fall set up a circular or oval path for their cruising. They appear to travel at random, but they usually return to the scene of a rise if you give them enough time. When another trout is rising just as sporadically a couple of long casts away, it might seem like a long time. But waiting patiently for a trout to expose its itinerary is the most likely way to hook fall trout that appear to be rising randomly.

You can fish for such trout in one of two ways. The first is to hold your fire and wait for a rise within range. That is best. You already know the general outlines of the trout's circuit, so you know roughly the direction it will take after its rise. Cast ahead of it with a dry, wet, nymph, or Woolly Bugger. If your fly is dry, just wait. If it's sunk, animate it when you feel the trout is close enough to have it in sight. You're going to hook that fish.

The second method is to place yourself somewhere on the trout's circuit, then cast and retrieve constantly across what you estimate to be its path. This works less well, because chances are half that you'll line the fish and spook it. The other half of the time you'll interest it, and an interested trout in fall is generally a hooked one.

Once you've caught that first trout by patiently waiting it out, then it's time to turn around, creep up on the second one, establish its path and its timing, and interest it. With patience and a little luck, you'll be able to catch it, too, and go on to scout out another.

This type of patient fishing on lakes, and the nymph and streamer fishing effective on streams in late fall, carry you on to winter, when the cycle of the four seasons of trout fishing does not end but is renewed.

INDEX